WU XING

Feng Shui

D1716742

Red Feather Mind, Body, Spirit
An imprint of Schiffer Publishing, Ltd.
4880 Lower Valley Road
Atglen, PA 19310
Phone: (610) 593-1777; Fax: (610) 593-2002
E-mail: Info@schifferbooks.com
Web: www.redfeathermbs.com

First published in 1998 by Eddison Sadd.

ISBN 978-0-7643-5886-9

10 9 8 7 6 5 4 3 2 1

Printed in China

WU XING

Feng Shui

REBALANCE
THE FLOW
OF ENERGY
IN AND
AROUND
YOU

REDFeather™

MIND | BODY | SPIRIT

4880 Lower Valley Road, Atglen, PA 19310

Contents

Introduction

Ch'i cannot be seen or heard but its influence can be found in all things, from the flow of a river to the peak of a mountain, and from a thriving shopping center to a quiet suburban street. *Ch'i* is the "life breath," or energy, that is continually gathering and dispersing, rising and falling, condensing and evaporating. *Feng shui* (pronounced "fung shway") is the art of understanding the flow of ch'i, of recognizing hidden forces in the land and in the cosmos—forces that may be in perfect harmony in one place but in complete disarray in another. Feng shui is also a way of looking at our environment that will be unfamiliar to many in the West: landforms are not simply static sites upon which we express our designs or needs, but are forms shaped by the flow of energy—forms that influence all life around them.

Feng shui is an ancient Chinese term that means "wind and water."

These are the elemental forces that shape and mould the landscape, seen in the movement of ch'i and the balance of yin and yang. All things in the universe are in a constant state of change, and yin and yang are the expression of this change. Yin is powerful, strong, hot and fiery while yang is luminous, watery, cool and dark; they are present in all patterns, activities, forms and emotions. A skilled feng shui practitioner reads the movement of ch'i and understands the balance of yin and yang, and is able to see how they are expressed across the landscape and assess their influence on a particular site.

Feng shui hinges on the belief that we recognize the existence of an intrinsic harmony, but that in certain places this harmony is disjointed or broken. Once the source of the problem has been identified, corrective measures can be taken to try to re-establish balance. Instead of being passive recipients we take an active and cooperative role in the workings of the world around us.

Using the Workbook

This easy-to-follow workbook explains the principles that govern feng shui and shows you how to "read" and understand your environment. It provides an essential guide to rural and urban landscapes that gives you the opportunity to assess important features both in and around your home and workplace, as well as to take appropriate steps to improve the feng shui where needed.

Part One introduces the philosophy of feng shui, beginning with the Tao, which is regarded as the ultimate source of all life. The forces of yin and yang and the energy of ch'i, so central to the practice of feng shui, arise from the harmony of the Tao and are described here to enable you to read their balance and effect in a particular area.

The process of change that is seen in the movement of yin and yang is represented by the eight trigrams of the I Ching, the ancient Chinese oracle that dates back thousands of years. Each trigram is associated with a direction of the compass as well as one of the five Chinese elements: this system provides the basis for your personal Pa Tzu compass readings which you can use to ensure that the elements are harmonious in your home. This early section of the book also introduces you to the idea of looking at the land as a dynamic and animate force endowed with beneficial or destructive qualities. In feng shui, the energy present in the land and water is reflected in the form of a dragon, and the qualities the dragon bestows upon natural features are also explored here. Many feng shui "problems" observed at a site can be resolved by implementing simple measures, and so this section includes general "solutions." These are the guidelines to using countermeasures to control the flow of ch'i or protect against destructive energy.

Once armed with your "tools"—an understanding of

how feng shui works, how to assess your environment and use your Pa Tzu compass, and how to make improvements—you are ready to move on to the practical section.

Part Two shows you—step by step—how to carry out readings for every aspect of your surroundings, from the location of your home to the layout of your living-room furniture. This highly visual section illustrates both positive and negative examples throughout and offers easy-to-follow advice whenever improvements are needed. So, starting from the outside and working in, we move from the rural landscape to road patterns, shape and position of buildings, plots of land, gardens and the entrance to a house or building. Once inside the home, you begin by assessing the overall layout and then working through each room in turn. Whether you want to check the size and position of furniture, doors and windows, or find out if your color scheme is in harmony with your personal element, there is something here to cater for everyone. Checklists offer helpful reminders of what to look out for in each room. And there is also advice on how to improve feng shui in the workplace, however limited the scope for improvement may be.

Whatever your situation, this indispensable guide shows you how feng shui can help you to change your life.

YOUR FENG SHUI TOOLS

Wisdom

This section introduces the principles of feng shui, explaining how it works and how to read feng shui in your environment. You can discover how to balance the five elements to establish harmony in your home and how to calculate your personal pa tzu compass to find your lucky and unlucky directions. General "remedies" for improving feng shui are also included in this section. Together, these are the "tools" you will be putting to practical use when you come to assess your surroundings in Part Two.

PART

1

The Principles of Feng Shui

The Tao

At its heart, feng shui is a way of working with the natural harmony, or order, of the universe—tao (or sometimes dao). *Tao* is often translated as "the way" or "path," a path that has been followed for centuries by sages and immortals. But tao has a more profound meaning—it is the ultimate source of all life.

Tao is the origin of all things that existed before creation. Although its ultimate nature is beyond form and language, tao is visibly expressed in the pattern of nature and the inter-dependency of all living things. Feng shui is a way of expressing our relation-ship with tao, a guide to living in harmony with this primordial energy.

Through feng shui, our relationship with the environment is not one of control or dominance but instead one of inter-relationship.

The patterns of change in the seasons, in the landscape, and in our emotions reflect the movement of tao. Just as a bright day may become overcast or a storm gives way to stillness, positive and negative aspects rise and fall; nothing is created or exists in isolation. Life flourishes, then decays to return to tao, and in the process of decay new life arises. Feng shui is a way of reading this process of change, of identifying areas of life-giving or decaying energy and actively balancing elements and correcting weaknesses.

Heaven, Earth, and Humanity

The triad of heaven, earth, and humanity is the traditional expression of tao, and it is frequently represented in Chinese landscape paintings. Towering mountain peaks, often shrouded in clouds, reach up to the sky, symbolizing the union of heaven and earth. Steep slopes are balanced by a gentler, greener landscape where water and land meet, a sign of flourishing earth energy. Scattered across the landscape are signs of human dwellings, people fishing, farming, or simply traveling along the mountain paths. The houses and temples blend harmoniously with the landscape, protected by its forms, completing the balance between heaven, earth, and humanity.

Yin and Yang

Yin and yang are natural forces that are present in all life, continually rising and falling, expanding or withdrawing. Yin and yang are in constant state of movement, and through this dynamic interplay, they create the changing pattern of life. Their interaction is clearly seen in the cycle of the seasons; yang is at its peak in the heat of summer while yin is at its weakest. As fall mists appear, yin begins its ascendency while yang starts to decline; by midwinter, yang has withdrawn while yin is powerful, but with the increasing warmth of spring, yang begins to expand once again.

Yin and yang are said to have been created at the beginning of time when everything was vague and formless. First, the universe was created out of this emptiness, and in its turn the universe created clear, light forces that drifted up to become heaven, while the heavy forces solidified to form the earth. According to the writings of Huai Nan Tzu (ca. 120 BCE):

ABOVE **The well-known yin/yang symbol represents the constantly changing patterns of life.**

The union of heaven, earth, and humanity are found in a traditional Chinese landscape. The mountains soar skyward while human activity flourishes below.

"The combined essences of heaven and earth became yin and yang, the concentrated essences of yin and yang became the four seasons, and the scattered essences of the four seasons became the myriad creatures of the world. After a long time, the hot forces of the accumulated yang produced fire and the essence of the fire force became the sun; the cold force of accumulated yin became water and the essence of the water force became the moon. The essence of the excess force of the sun and moon became the stars and planets. Heaven received the sun, moon, and stars while earth received water and soil."

(Huai Nan Tzu, quoted in *Sources of Chinese Tradition Vol. I*, edited by Theodore de Bary)

Yin and yang are most commonly described as opposite, dynamic forces. Yang is male and yin is female; yang is hot and yin is cold; yang is anger and yin is withdrawal; yang is activity and yin is stillness; yang is sharp and yin is soft.

In feng shui, however, yin and yang take on additional and different dimensions. The landscape in feng shui is categorized as land or water. Land is still and yin, whereas water is active and yang, which is why the ideal site combines hills and rivers. These two categories of the yin mountain and yang water are further subdivided according to the nature of the mountain (steep or gently undulating) or the nature of the water (stormy or still).

For example, craggy peaks are yin but flattop mountains are yang, and steep cliffs are yin but gentle slopes are yang. The yang aspects are more productive and dynamic while the yin aspects can be dangerous or destructive. Still water gathers energy and is yang, but fast-flowing water disperses energy and is yin; rivers that follow an irregular and sharply turning course are yin, but an evenly flowing meandering river is yang, because it produces positive energy. When water spurts out of the earth, it is yin, but it is yang when it seeps into the earth to nourish underground streams. Nothing is completely yin or yang, because these forces continually interact, thus there is always an element of yin in yang and yang in yin.

This dynamic relationship is central to feng shui, and an understanding of yin and yang is vital if you are to make a true assessment of your surroundings.

A site where steep cliffs meet stormy waters is powerfully yin. The energy here is destructive and you would be advised against choosing to live in this location.

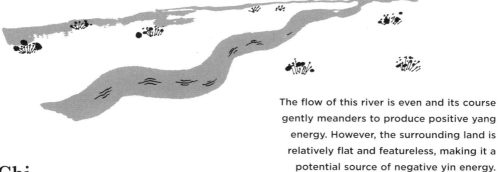

The flow of this river is even and its course gently meanders to produce positive yang energy. However, the surrounding land is relatively flat and featureless, making it a potential source of negative yin energy.

Chi

The life-giving breath or energy that shapes and animates all life is known as chi. It is continually moving and changing. The places where it gathers produce positive energy and the sites where it disperses allow negative energy to settle. You can channel chi to condense at a particular place, thereby enhancing the site's fortune, but if there is no room for movement, it will become trapped. In an open, featureless area, there is nothing to hold chi, so it sweeps across the land and will soon evaporate. At a more detailed level, a piece of furniture can block the flow of chi or it can quickly escape through an open door. In most cases you can regulate and control chi flow to prevent negative forces draining away the life energy.

In addition to the chi that courses through the land and rivers, and the chi that accumulates and disperses at certain points on the ground, there is also heaven chi. This is the chi that governs the cycle of the seasons and is closely identified with yin and yang. Heaven chi is divided into twenty-four phases, which mark the climatic and agricultural patterns of the year. The first phase is *Li Chun* (Beginning of Spring), a time when yin is declining and yang is ascending. The middle of the year is marked by *Ta Shu* (Great Heat), when yang is at its peak, and the year ends at *Ta Han* (Great Cold), when yin is at its most powerful.

Sha: The Life-taking Breaths

Chi that flows through and over the land is also subject to weakness and decay. When it is dispersed or blocked, its positive energy is drained and *sha,* or life-taking breaths, are allowed to enter. Sha produces negative or destructive energy; for example, the accumulation of refuse is a source of sha, as is stagnant water or rotting vegetation. Sha is also felt in bitterly cold winds that pierce gaps between buildings. It can travel along straight lines, such as electric power lines, arrowlike roads, and railroad lines, or it can be directed from the sharp corner of a building or natural feature. In most instances, you can take corrective action to remove, block, or deflect the source of sha, thereby allowing chi to reestablish itself.

The Trigrams

The continual interaction and tension between yin and yang creates the pattern of movement and change in the universe, a pattern ordained by tao. This never-ending cycle is reflected in the eight trigrams of I Ching. Each trigram is made up of three lines, which can be broken (a yin line) or unbroken (a yang line). One trigram has only yin lines while another has only yang; the remainder are a mixture of yin and yang. They are ordered in a circle to reflect the gradual movement from absolute yin to absolute yang, and back to absolute yin in a continuous cycle (see page 17).

If you look at the main pa tzu compass on page 32, you will see the eight trigrams positioned in their circular formation, each trigram relating to a particular element and direction. The order the trigrams follow is known as the Later Heaven sequence, and this is the order used on traditional feng shui compasses to show the balance and movement of yin and yang on the ground. (There is another sequence known as Former Heaven, which follows a different order that represents the annual cycle of yin and yang through the seasons; this sequence is a reflection of the cosmic forces of yin and yang.)

The Trigram Associations

Trigram	Direction	Natural Phenomenon	Attributes	Member of Family
Li	south	fire	adherence, dependence	middle daughter
Kun	southwest	earth	receptive, yielding	mother
Tui	west	lake	joy, serenity	youngest daughter
Chien	northwest	heaven	creative, strong	father
Kan	north	water	danger, flowing water	middle son
Ken	northeast	mountain	steadiness, stillness	youngest son
Chen	east	thunder	arousing movement	eldest son
Sun	southeast	wind	penetration, gentleness	eldest daughter

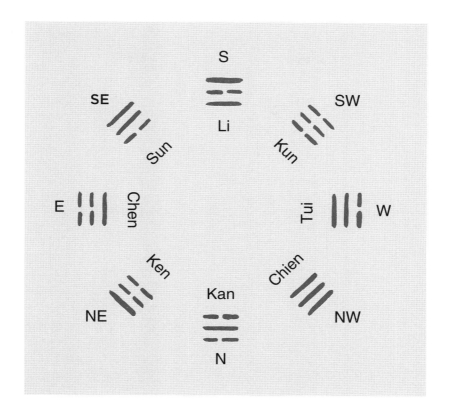

The top line of the trigrams is on the outside and the lower line on the inside. South is at the top of this sequence, because Chinese compasses are orientated south–north.

The trigrams have universal associations, including natural phenomena and attributes, among other things, and some of these are listed in the chart on the previous page.

The Five Elements

The five elements of wood, fire, earth, metal, and water are used in traditional Chinese arts to describe the process of change. They exist to a greater or lesser extent in all substances, and their interaction illustrates the continual growth and decay within the universe. According to the *Shu Ching* (Book of History), heaven decreed the order of the universe and the first plan was to divide all phenomena into five elements:

"The nature of water is to soak and descend; of fire, to blaze and ascend; of wood, to be crooked and to be straight; of metal to obey and to change; while the virtue of earth is seen in seed sowing and ingathering. That which soaks and descends becomes salt; that which blazes and ascends becomes bitter; that which is crooked and straight becomes sour; that which obeys and changes becomes acrid; and from seedsowing and ingathering becomes sweetness."

(The Great Plan, from *The Chinese Classics Vol. III,* translated by James Legge)*

The elements exist in a continual cycle of creation and destruction: some create, feed, and strengthen, while others weaken, dissipate, and destroy. This is a necessary process, however, because each interaction leads to a new element. The flux and opposition of yin and yang are also seen in their movement: for example, when the element of water is stagnant, it is yin; when it is clean and flowing smoothly, it is yang; and when it is stormy and dangerous, it is once again yin. The effect of the interaction of the elements and how to interpret them in a reading is discussed in more detail on pages 26–31.

The dragon is identified in the shape of the land, and the chi that flows over and through the land is known as the dragon's blood.

The Dragon

In feng shui practice, the shapes of the land, the flow of rivers, and the patterns created by light and wind are associated with a variety of animal forms. These animals bestow a quality on the land that can be dynamic, energetic, or dangerous. Of all the animals, however, the dragon is the most important landform, identifiable in virtually every topographical feature. It is seen in linear shapes, and ridges, hilltops, slopes, hills, and valleys are all veins of the dragon and the source of the dragon's breath. The chi that courses through the land is known as the dragon's blood. The dragon is also seen in the pattern of watercourses, where it is known as the Water Dragon; the rivers are the dragon's ducts along which chi is channeled (see page 54).

The dragon is, therefore, more than just a metaphor for mountains and rivers—it is actually an animate presence that carries life-giving energy. The dragon's veins vary from kingly to ordinary—from powerful majestic peaks, a range of mountain ridges, and sweeping valleys to a small range of low rolling hills. The dragon's presence can be dangerous if the mountain ridges end abruptly and steeply, because chi cannot be absorbed gently into the

land. The dragon's form should build up from spread out lower veins to higher peaks that stretch out to create a long spine, and then slowly spread out once again into lower ridges.

There are also many variations of the dragon's form; some hold dynamic energy for centuries, giving them the ability to sustain repeated use, while others cannot regenerate once they have been used for building. Some dragon forms are deep and concentrated sources of energy; others are less intensive and their energy is diffused. (See page 53 for examples of dynamic animal forms.)

Often the power of a mountain is enhanced by water flowing across its veins. When water flows steadily toward a dynamic mountain, the energies gather to generate great power—the mountain concentrates the water energy while the water spreads the mountain energy—but water flowing swiftly from a site will weaken and drain those energies.

As the water flows swiftly away from the site toward the sea, the dragon's energy is drained. The chi that was concentrated in the dragon's form on this mountain changes abruptly as it rolls forcefully down the steep cliffs.

Wind

Wind is another carrier of energy. Sharp cold winds cutting through cracks, blowing over ridges, or racing across plains carry destructive energy, while gentle breezes animate and spread chi. Wind blowing across a mountain range sometimes travels like an arrow piercing gaps and valleys, but if the dragon's veins in the mountain are balanced, they control the wind and channel it toward the site.

Sites on open hills or plains need protection from vegetation or buildings to control the impact of wind flow and protect the site. In contrast, a site that is completely overshadowed or enclosed could become a source of sha, because there is no movement to activate chi. A balance has to be established so that the site is not vulnerable to adverse weather conditions yet is open enough to benefit from natural light and warmth.

Although this house is isolated, the wind is channeled through the valleys toward the site at the center and its flow is balanced by the protective hills around the site.

Landform Energy

When a site is weak or vulnerable, a large structure can help to balance or protect it, although obviously the structure will not have had the time to absorb the primordial energy of the universe that is an inherent part of most landforms. When mountains are leveled, valleys flooded, or quarries built, the deep source of energy that has been accumulated over millennia is cut, swept away, or destroyed. Likewise, the construction of large-scale power stations or dams disturb, weaken, and often destroy a dynamic site. When natural disasters occur, such as volcanic eruptions, earthquakes, or landslides, the earth's energy is abruptly forced out and new landforms may result. Some may block the path of energy and others may channel energy effectively, although these new landforms have not had enough time to become deep sources of energy.

The Four Animal Guardians

Every site, whether urban or rural, is surrounded by four animal spirits: the Black Tortoise, Red Bird, Green Dragon, and White Tiger. In its early history, feng shui was developed to determine auspicious sites for burial so the spirits of the ancestors were calmed and protected. These four animals were the guardians around the grave and their position was—and still is— determined from the position of the grave itself looking outward to the Red Bird, backed behind by the Black Tortoise, with the Green Dragon to the left and the White Tiger to the right. In feng shui, burial sites belong to the yin domain (see page 23).

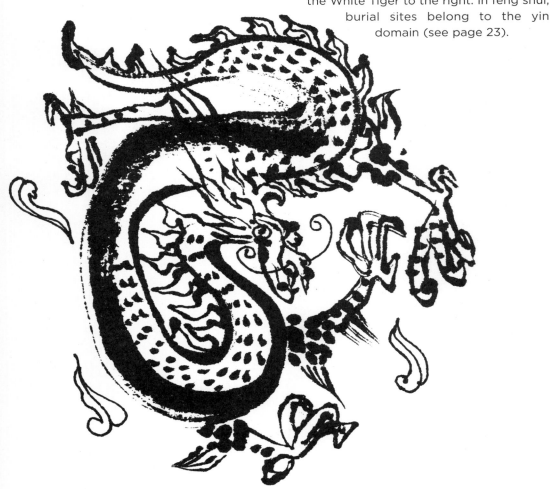

The animal spirits that surround residential or commercial buildings are determined from a different perspective, because these buildings belong to the yang domain. When taking a reading, the observer stands outside, facing toward the front of the building. The Red Bird is at the front of the site, the Black Tortoise at the back, the Green Dragon on the left, and the White Tiger on the right (see page 25). The role of the four animal guardians in protecting rural sites is discussed in more detail on page 52, and it features throughout the book in relation to examples of good and bad feng shui sites.

BELOW The yin-domain animal formation is applied to burial sites to make sure that the spirits of the ancestors are protected and can rest peacefully.

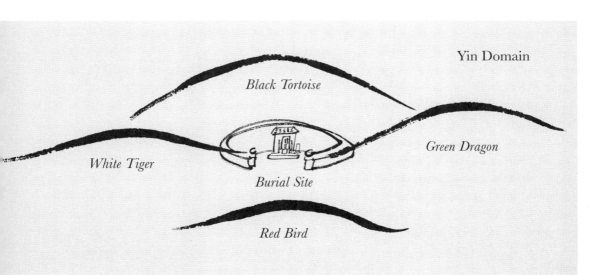

Using this Knowledge

Each of the principles outlined in this section plays a role in building up an understanding of a site. In Part Two, a wide range of sites are illustrated that provide immediate guidance, but the information on feng shui principles gives you a deeper understanding of how and why these guidelines were created.

If you are doing a reading of a specific feature, it cannot be taken in isolation from the surrounding environment. For example, the feng shui of a house is first of all affected by the site: Is it on a hillside or in a valley? Is it subject to powerful yin or yang forces? Is it on a site where the dragon is powerful? If you live in an urban area, buildings often take the place of natural features, so taller buildings at the rear of a house, in the position of the Black Tortoise, offer

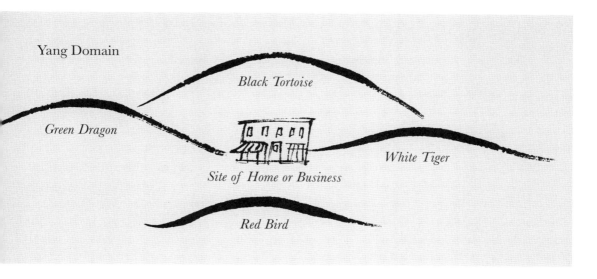

Yang Domain

Black Tortoise

Green Dragon

Site of Home or Business

White Tiger

Red Bird

ABOVE **The yang-domain animal formation applies to homes and businesses. This is the formation you will need to account for when you assess your surroundings.**

the protection that a hill might provide in a rural area. Similarly, heavy and fast-moving traffic in front of your house will dissipate energy in the same way that the strong current of a fast-flowing river will disperse chi.

It is important to build up a picture that takes account of both large- and small-scale factors, because a strength in one area might help to offset a weakness in another. It is inevitable that some features simply cannot be changed, but you will find that it is always possible to use a variety of tools to create a more balanced and harmonious site.

The Five Elements

The Chinese call the five elements *wu xing*; *wu* means "five" and *xing* means "to go" or "to move." Although the five elements are classified as wood, fire, earth, metal, and water, they are essentially a way of referring to the movements, actions, and changes that take place at every level of life.

The elements are not static but are continually nourishing each other or overpowering one another. They are types of energy that shape and transform all life, and they are present in everything, although one element may be more dominant than the others. The elements are reflected in shapes, forms, textures, colors, directions, health, and patterns of change, which is why they are important to understanding and practicing feng shui. Also, when you begin to analyze a floor plan of a room or a house, you will need to be familiar with the elements to be able to improve and strengthen a weak area.

The Cycles of the Elements

The interaction of the elements can be productive or destructive—some elements overpower each other and some produce each other. For example, when water is powerful, it overwhelms and extinguishes fire, but if fire is powerful, it reduces objects to ashes to produce earth. This process is summed up by saying water destroys fire and fire produces earth.

In this productive cycle, wood burns to produce heat and the upward movement of fire. Fire then consumes objects, turning them to ashes to produce earth. The nourishing quality of the earth produces metal and, in turn, the metal in the earth enriches underground water. Water rises to the surface to feed vegetation and thus to produce wood, and so the cycle of production continues (see page 27).

In this destructive cycle, wood covers and penetrates the earth, constricting and taking nourishment from it. In its turn, earth controls the direction and flow of streams and rivers. Water overcomes the flames and heat of fire and ultimately extinguishes it. Fire weakens and then melts metal, and the sharp, cutting power of metal can destroy wood (see page 27), thus beginning the cycle once again.

When you start to read about the feng shui of a room or house using the pa tzu compass, it is important to know how these elements combine with each other. Every direction has an element associated with it, and you also have your own personal element (which you will discover when you reach pages 32–37). You will need to know whether your element works in harmony with, or clashes with, the element of the particular direction you are assessing. If your element is harmonious, you have a positive reading; however, if it clashes, you will need to improve the reading by following the suggested remedial methods.

The productive cycle of the five elements is shown in the outer circle, while the inner pentagram shows the destructive cycle of the five elements.

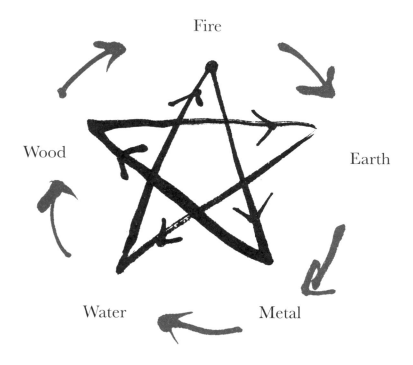

Productive cycle	Destructive cycle
Wood produces fire	Wood destroys earth
Fire produces earth	Earth destroys water
Earth produces metal	Water destroys fire
Metal produces water	Fire destroys metal
Water produces wood	Metal destroys wood

Universal Associations

Over the centuries, the elements have been linked with numerous features, such as planets, tastes, weather conditions, parts of the body, and domestic animals (see below). The system of matching the five elements has been developed to such an extent that they can be correlated to almost anything in the universe. Because the elements are at the heart of all the processes of change, their wide-ranging associations can be used in a variety of divinational and medicinal practices, from astrology to Chinese herbal medicine.

Element Associations

Element	Planet	Taste	Weather	Organ	Animal
WOOD	Jupiter	sourness	wind	spleen	sheep
FIRE	Mars	bitterness	heat	lungs	poultry
EARTH	Saturn	sweetness	sunshine	heart	ox
METAL	Venus	acridity	cold	kidney	dog
WATER	Mercury	saltiness	rain	liver	pig

The Five Elements and Yin and Yang

The dynamic tension of yin and yang is also seen in the five elements. Yang is at its peak in the heat and light of fire, and although it is still relatively strong, it is less powerful in the growth and productivity of wood. On the other hand, yin is at its peak in the cold and damp qualities of water, while it is strong but less dominant in the malleable qualities of metal. The forces of yin and yang are equally balanced and harmonious in the element of earth.

Using the Elements to Improve Your Feng Shui

When you begin to analyze a floor plan of a room, you may find that certain elements clash—one element may need to be strengthened or the overpowering one may need to be channeled in another direction. To be able to improve your feng shui, you will need to know how to introduce, or diminish, each of the elements, and the colors and objects listed on page 30 will help you to do so.

For example, if the fire element is too powerful in your bedroom, it could cause sleepless nights. First, you need to check how fire can be controlled according to the elemental cycles: fire produces earth; fire destroys metal; and water destroys fire.

The power of fire can be diminished by the element of water, so the introduction of a clear glass vase of flowers, a bowl of water, or paintings of water scenes will weaken fire. You can also use the color black in fabrics or ornaments, but do not overwhelm the room with black. Or you can weaken fire by directing it toward colors, textures, and objects associated with earth; if the element of earth is increased, fire will be weakened as it works to feed and create earth. And, because fire destroys metal, the introduction of metal colors and objects will challenge and dissipate fire. However, do not let elements attack each other too forcefully when using the destructive cycle.

The elemental colors can be used in a variety of ways, from cushions, curtains, blinds, paint, or wallpaper to furniture or ornaments. Rooms do not necessarily need to be dominated by one color—often the introduction of that color through one or two items will help to establish balance.

Wood

Fire

Earth

Metal

Water

Element and Color

WOOD

Wood can be shaped and formed and is associated with relaxation.

Color: Green. All shades of green can be used, from pale green to lime green, sea green, mid-green, and dark green.

FIRE

Fire has burning and ascending qualities and is associated with enlightenment.

Color: Red. Various shades, ranging from deep orange and pink to fiery red, deep red, purple, and burgundy, can be used.

EARTH

Earth has productive and creative qualities and is associated with care and attention.

Color: Yellow. Colors that range from light orange to pale lemon hues and from bright yellow to a warm golden color can be used.

METAL

Metal has malleable qualities and is associated with energy.

Color: White. Shades that range from pale grays and off-white to bright white and cream can be used.

WATER

Water has qualities of soaking and descending and is associated with peace and quiet.

Color: Black. Dark colors, such as dark gray, deep blue, or indigo, to various hues of black can be used.

How to Introduce an Element into a Room

- Wooden furniture, such as tables, chairs, or stools. Wood can also be incorporated into furniture designs and paneling, or it can be used for shutters or blinds made of bamboo or wooden slats. Wood is also present in raffia and chipboard, although the wood element is most powerful in solid wood itself.
- Ornaments, such as letter or paper racks, jewelry or storage boxes, wooden sculptures, wooden bowls, and dishes, vases, or picture frames.
- Plants are a strong source of wood, particularly if they have woody stems. Bonsai trees, flowerpot plants, and fresh or dry flower arrangements can all be used.

- Fire and heat are natural sources of this element. A "real" fire is the most powerful source, but fire is also strong in gas and electric heaters.
- Light is a source of fire, whether it is a table lamp or ceiling light, and if there is a fan attached to the light, the fire element is further strengthened and circulated.
- Paintings, drawings, or photographs that depict fire, heat, or sunshine can all be used, as well as sculptures or ornaments that symbolize fire or heat.

- Earth itself in ceramic pots increases this element, as do yellow flowers, but be careful to avoid using plants with woody stems, because wood destroys earth in the destructive elemental cycle.
- Plain clay vases, flowerpots, or ornaments are also sources of the earth element, as are ceramic vases, bowls, tiles, and china.
- Earth can also be depicted in paintings or drawings, but be aware that other elements may also be present in images, such as water or wood.

- Metal itself can be used in furniture or fittings as well as in ornaments. Metal vases, sculptures, candlesticks, cutlery, tools, or picture frames will all strengthen the element. If you do use metal candlesticks, remember that fire is introduced if you light the candle.
- Clocks with a swinging pendulum are a useful source of metal, because they introduce the element as well as increase its effectiveness through regular constant movement.

- Water in a clear vase is a strong source for this element, but do not let the water become dirty or stagnant. Clear glass is particularly good for holding water because it resembles ice, which is also a source of water energy. Water is strengthened in fountains or aquariums, because the movement of the water increases its energy.
- Water can be depicted in drawings or paintings, but avoid stormy scenes, such as hurricanes, or scenes of stagnant water, because both are powerfully yin.

The Pa Tzu Compass

The pa tzu compass is the guide to discovering your personal element. There are nine directions on the pa tzu compass, including the center, and each one corresponds to a number, trigram, element, and category known as Eastern or Western life, represented here by the letters E and W (see below). This compass follows the traditional Chinese south–north orientation.

How to Find Your Pa Tzu Number

The number that belongs to you depends on the year of your birth. After you determine your number (go through the calculations on page 33), you can find out which element and trigram is associated with your character. This number is also the key to your personal compass, which follows a north–south orientation.

Now that you know your number, you can find your pa tzu compass. The eight "mini" compasses, which come from the main pa tzu compass shown below, are divided into two groups called Eastern Life and Western Life. If your number is 1, 3, 4, or 9, you belong to the Eastern Life group. Your lucky directions are east, southeast, north, and south. If your number is 2, 6, 7, or 8, you belong to the Western Life group. Your lucky directions are west, southwest, northwest, and northeast. If your number is 5, you should use compass 2 if you are male and compass 8 if you are female, because 5 represents the center and does not have its own compass.

Man   女   Woman

Calculations for Men

- Subtract the last two numbers of your year of birth from 100 and divide by 9.
- The remainder is the number of your compass.
- If there is no remainder, you should take the number 9.
  Example: Born in 1962
  $$100 - 62 = 38$$
  $$38 \div 9 = 4 \text{ remainder } 2$$
  Your number is 2.

Calculations for Women

- Subtract 4 from the last two numbers of your year of birth and divide by 9.
- The remainder is the number of your compass.
- If there is no remainder, you should take the number 9.
  Example: Born in 1962
  $$62 - 4 = 58$$
  $$58 \div 9 = 6 \text{ remainder } 4$$
  Your number is 4.

Compass Categories

Each of the eight pa tzu compasses has four positive and four negative directions that cover different aspects of your fortune. On the traditional pa tzu compass, the unlucky directions are called Five Ghosts, Death, Disaster, and Unlucky Influences. These categories are not as foreboding as they sound, so they are represented here by the names Loss, Illness, Disagreement, and Indecision respectively, which are more appropriate to their meanings.

The unlucky categories represent the possibility of negative fortune, but the weakness that lies in these areas can be corrected by introducing one or more of the five elements, as appropriate. Essentially, the categories mark the division of good and bad fortune, but they can also be linked to the aspects of life listed on the right:

- Life covers prosperity in relation to your family and career.
- Good Fortune relates to success in ideas, projects, and contacts.
- Vitality relates to energy and general well-being.
- Longevity is linked to health and long life.
- Loss relates to the loss of objects, projects, or finance.
- Illness covers lack of energy, tiredness, as well as general ailments.
- Disagreement relates to setbacks and unexpected events.
- Indecision covers disappointments, delays, and unforeseen difficulties.

Pa Tzu Compasses: Eastern Life

Pa Tzu Compass
No. 1

Element: Water
Trigram: Kan

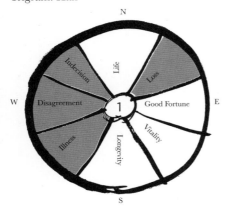

Pa Tzu Compass
No. 4

Element: Wood
Trigram: Sun

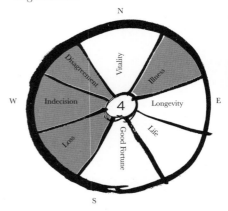

☐ Lucky
directions

■ Unlucky
directions

Pa Tzu Compass
No. 3

Element: Wood
Trigram: Chen

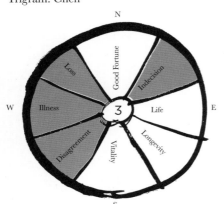

Pa Tzu Compass
No. 9

Element: Fire
Trigram: Li

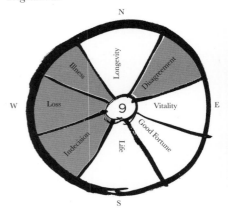

Pa Tzu Compasses: Western Life

Pa Tzu Compass
No. 2

Element: Earth
Trigram: Kun

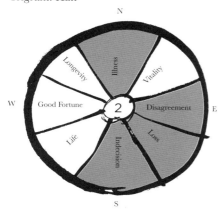

Pa Tzu Compass
No. 7

Element: Metal
Trigram: Tui

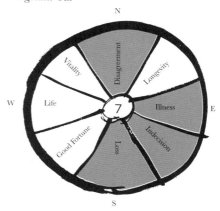

Pa Tzu Compass
No. 6

Element: Metal
Trigram: Chien

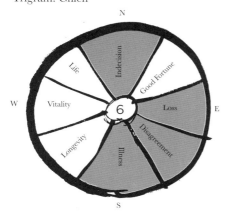

Pa Tzu Compass
No. 8

Element: Earth
Trigram: Ken

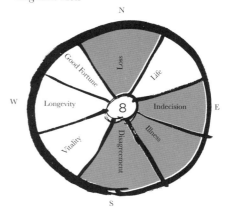

Lucky
directions

Unlucky
directions

Using Your Compass

In Part Two, you will find general feng shui guidelines for particular areas in and around your home and workplace, but in addition to following these guidelines, you can also analyze the floor plan of your home or the layout of specific rooms to discover how they relate to your own year of birth. This is when you refer to your personal pa tzu compass. To take a reading, all you need to know are your element and your lucky and unlucky directions (simply follow the calculations on page 33).

Each direction is associated with one of the five elements, and these always remain the same (see below). As we have already seen, some elements combine positively while others combine negatively. By using your pa tzu compass to take a reading, you can find out which areas of your home or workplace need improving by checking how the element of the direction you are assessing combines with the element of your pa tzu compass.

The easiest way to use your compass is to draw a basic floor plan of the area or room you want to assess (drawing it as accurately to scale as possible), and then draw your compass on top. You might find it helpful to draw your compass on a piece of tracing paper, so that you can simply overlay it on your floor plan, instead of drawing a new compass every time you want to take a reading. The important thing to remember is that you must always align the north point of your compass with the northerly direction of the area you are assessing. Alternatively, you could stand in the center of the area or room and use the compass printed in this book, pointing north on your pa tzu compass toward the northerly direction of the room.

If the room is an irregular shape, some sections of the compass will not be completely covered. Do not try to adjust the reading by moving your position or by moving the compass; just work within the space allocated to each direction.

Each direction is associated with an element, and this pairing always remains the same.

Shared Accommodation

If you live alone, you need to use only your personal compass; if you are part of a family, you should use the compass belonging to the main breadwinner. Each family member will, however, be able to carry out a reading for his or her bedroom or study. If you rent a house and there are several people living there, you should focus your reading on your bedroom or apartment. The pa tzu compass helps to give you a more personalized reading, but there are also many general feng shui principles illustrated in the following sections that can help you understand the practice of feng shui.

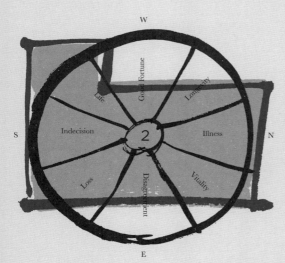

By overlaying your pa tzu compass on a floor plan, you can discover where the weaknesses lie and which elements need to be strengthened or diminished.

Example

In the illustration on the left, pa tzu compass number 2 has been overlaid on a floor plan of a room. This compass belongs to the Western Life group, which means that the unlucky directions are north, east, southeast, and south. These are the directions where the weaknesses lie, so you need to check how your pa tzu element (in this case, earth) combines with the elements of these directions (water, wood, wood, and fire respectively). The elemental cycles show that earth destroys water, wood destroys earth, and fire produces earth, so therefore the directions that require the most attention in this example are the east and southeast.

It is important that your pa tzu element is not overwhelmed in the negative areas, so you need to strengthen or diminish the elements as appropriate, using the advice on pages 29–31.

Feng Shui Solutions: Protecting a Site

There are several subtle but effective ways of dealing with negative energy traveling toward your home, of counteracting the effect of slow-moving chi or of energizing an area where chi is blocked. Sometimes the feng shui of a room can be improved simply by altering the arrangement of your furniture, by introducing greenery, or by improving the lighting conditions. In other instances, architectural or natural features may be channeling destructive energy into your home and you may need to use a range of tools, such as mirrors, blinds, screens, greenery, colors, and light, all of which can be employed to offer protection and add balance.

The way in which you deal with negative energy depends on the force you are trying to counteract. Destructive energy can be blocked with blinds or screens, reflected with mirrors, absorbed by soft material, or bounced back with springs. This section guides you through a range of tools and how they can be used to protect a site and enhance chi in a particular area.

Any reflective surface—even a polished wok or aluminum foil—can be used instead of a mirror to achieve the desired effect.

Mirrors

Traditionally, mirrors have been one of the most popular and effective feng shui tools. They continue to be widely used as a way to deflect malign forces and negative energy directed at a building or particular features. They are especially effective in reflecting back harmful energy channeled down knifelike roads or carried like an arrow from power lines or the pointed corner of a building. They also deflect the potentially detrimental effects from oncoming traffic, harmful reflections, sharp corners of natural features or roads, and the angular points of architectural features.

You should hang mirrors in line with the force approaching the building so they reflect the attacking object. For example, if you are protecting yourself from the powerful onrush of chi traveling down a straight road, the mirror should be large enough for the road to be reflected on its surface. The branch of a dead tree or the eaves of a roof pointing at a bedroom window might only need a small ornamental mirror.

Mirrors are also effective in activating slow-moving chi or energizing areas where chi may be blocked, because they reflect light and increase the feeling of space. For example, a mirror in a long, narrow corridor will reflect back and enhance the energy of this area, or a mirror at the foot of basement stairs will help to bring yang into a yin area. When you are positioning mirrors, be careful so that part of your head is not cut off in the reflection; this is particularly relevant when the mirror is placed near the top or bottom of a staircase.

While mirrors are strong reflectors and enhancers, their effect can be overwhelming or startling if they are hung either opposite each other, directly in the line of open doors or large windows, or at the foot of the bed. Chi coming in through a door or window needs a chance to circulate and should not be immediately reflected back, while a mirror at the foot of a bed can give you an unexpected shock if you wake up suddenly.

Mirrors help to energize areas where chi may be sluggish or move slowly—they increase the feeling of space and light.

Powerful gods, such as this
god of the north shown here,
are traditionally depicted
underneath pa kua mirrors to
help deflect malign spirits.

Pa Kua Mirrors

The traditional feng shui mirror is called a *pa kua* mirror, and these can be bought at most Chinese supermarkets. They are small, round mirrors set in a red wooden frame (in China, the color red is associated with good fortune and prosperity). Below the mirror there is often a colorful painting of the god of the north (see left) or the fearsome god of war, both of whom are believed to ward off unlucky spirits. Around the mirror itself are the eight trigrams of I Ching in the positions of the eight directions (see page 16 for the interpretation of the trigrams). The order of the trigrams follows the Former Heaven sequence—the earlier, alternative sequence to the trigrams that appear in the pa tzu system (the pa tzu compass follows the Later Heaven sequence). When reading these trigrams, the top line of the trigram is on the outside and the lower line on the inside.

Pa kua mirrors are usually hung above the front door of houses, restaurants, or offices, but they can also be hung inside buildings. This traditional-style mirror is a popular feng shui tool, but you can use any mirror or reflective surface, such as a pan, wok, polished piece of metal, aluminum foil, bowl, or pool of water.

Vegetation

Vegetation is an indication of healthy chi in and above the ground. It can have energizing and calming effects as well as be a useful means of strengthening and protecting a site. If one of the four animal spirits is weak around a building, trees or bushes can give additional support, or if your house is in a flat, featureless area, vegetation will help to prevent the dispersal of chi and accumulation of sha. Trees and bushes also act as screens to shield a building from fast-flowing chi on steep slopes or protect it from swift-moving traffic or the pressure created by corners of walls or other buildings.

Flowers and plants also play their role in activating chi on small balconies, patios, and in the home or office. However, if you are introducing plants or flowers into a room, change the water regularly to prevent it from becoming stagnant, keep the soil watered, and remove flowers or leaves if they begin to wilt. The same rule applies to the vegetation outside your home—a healthy green tree produces positive energy but a dead tree can be a source of negative energy.

If you are using vegetation to balance, protect, and shield an area, do not overcrowd the space or plant so that the roots undermine the building. While trees are an indication of nourishing chi, if they overwhelm a house, blocking out the light and preventing the growth of other vegetation, they have an oppressive effect. You should also avoid random planting, because one well-sited tree can be more effective than a row of trees and bushes clumped together; evergreen trees are especially useful for single planting, because they keep their cover.

Colors

There are no absolute rules on how or where colors should be used, although the guidelines in the section on the five elements (see pages 30–31) will help you to create a balance and use color to strengthen your personal element. There may be colors that make you feel uneasy, while others create a relaxing atmosphere, so you should also follow your personal preference.

A balanced use of color enhances the feng shui of a room and creates a sense of harmony, whereas the excessive use of one color can create an uneasy atmosphere. For example, an all-red room introduces a powerful fire element and may eventually make the occupants tense and argumentative. Because white is traditionally linked to mourning, an all-white room is considered unlucky and is also closely associated with hospitals and clinics. If you want to use one color as the main one for a room, introduce other colors through textures, fabrics, or ornaments so that one element does not dominate the room.

You can use trees and plants to activate chi, strengthen and protect a site, or screen against negative effects. They should not be overwhelming, however, and must always be kept healthy.

Blinds, Curtains, and Porches

If you need to protect your home or office from roads or the cutting effect of corners, or from traffic traveling close by, you can create a barrier with blinds or curtains. The effect shields your house from negative or oppressive energy and gives you a layer of protection. If the front door is subject to destructive forces, a porch can also serve this purpose, particularly if the entrance is moved to the side, away from the direct line of the front door.

Blinds and curtains are also used to prevent a disproportionate amount of chi entering a room. This principle applies for floor-to-ceiling single-pane windows or for windows that run the full length of the room, because their size and position may let excessive sunlight or cold enter the room.

Blinds (above) can be used as a barrier, while paintings (below) can invoke an atmosphere or strengthen an element. Springs (page 43) can bounce away negative energy.

Pictures and Symbols

Paintings, photographs, and drawings can all be used to create an atmosphere of activity, liveliness, or relaxation. Fertile landscapes are particularly useful, because they depict nourishing energy, whereas a scarred or stunted landscape indicates an absence of life-giving chi. A picture can also be used to strengthen an element when you are using the pa tzu system. For example, a waterfall or river will increase the water element, or a painting of a red sunset or burning leaves will improve the fire element. Images linked with violence, decay, or death depict destructive forces, so avoid hanging them in your home, where the emphasis should be on harmony and balance.

Sculptures, Textures, and Household Objects

Depending on the nature of the force you have to combat, sculptures, textures, and household objects can all be effective tools. For example, if the branches of a dead tree are pointing toward your house, you could place the blade of a saw outside your home, because it has a cutting effect on the attacking force. If you use a real saw, be careful to make sure that it is placed well out of children's reach; alternatively, a safer option is simply to use a model of a saw, or to file down the sharp teeth. The powerful energy of television or satellite antennae can be absorbed by materials, such as sand, foam, or wood chips, placed in an open basket, container, or tray. Springs positioned on the roof or outside your home or office help to ward off the effect of overpowering buildings or angular structures by bouncing back their incoming force. In these examples, you should place the tools in line with the attacking object so they will be effective.

When you are thinking of ways to protect part of a building from a negative force, take time to study the nature of the force. If you are trying to counteract the effect of sharp architectural features, telephone wires, electric lines, or antennae, you can soften and absorb their impact on your home. The effect of taller buildings, sharp corners, or roads directed at your home can also be bounced off so that the force is broken up into a variety of directions. If you are protecting your house or apartment from shapes that resemble weapons or animals ready to attack, either in the landscape or on buildings, you can protect the site by using pointed or cutting objects. (You should use models or sculptures to avoid accidents.)

Many Chinese homes or businesses have a fish tank or aquarium, because fish are thought to denote good fortune and healthy finance; the Chinese word for "fish" (*yu*) sounds similar to that for "excess" (*yu*).

Water

Water has strong life-giving qualities that encourage and nourish the flow of chi, but if it is low-lying or stagnant, it then becomes a source of sha—malign energy. Fresh flowers in a glass vase can enliven the flow of sluggish or blocked chi in a room, while a fountain in a lobby or foyer attracts beneficial chi into the building. A fish pond or ornamental pool in a front yard is also said to attract good fortune from distant places. The gentle movement of water is life-giving and yang—this is seen in the flow of a river or the smooth swell of the sea—but when water is hit by violent storms or becomes stagnant, it has strong yin qualities and can be destructive. This same principle applies to ponds, pools, and aquariums. Healthy plant life that improves the aeration of the water, or fish moving through the water, enliven chi and have yang qualities.

Curves and Symmetry

Circles and round structures are a sign of something that is complete as well as being an indication of satisfaction and happiness. Round structures or architectural features enable chi to flow evenly and smoothly, whereas sharp features can pierce chi and cluttered spaces break its flow.

If you are designing a yard, buying a house, or choosing furniture, aim for curves and balance so that an overall symmetry is created. While it is not always

possible to find accommodation with domed roofs, features such as curved paths, window frames, porches, or arches all enhance the flow of energy around the site. Complete shapes also provide more positive readings than irregular designs. For example, a rectangular or square plot of land is preferable to one that has sides of different lengths, while a room with two bays is more balanced than one with one narrow extension. Sometimes a structure can accommodate unusual shapes or uneven sections if it creates an overall impression of balance and proportion and relates harmoniously to the landforms around it.

Rounded, symmetrical furniture encourages a smooth flow of chi around a room.

Wind Chimes

Wind chimes were traditionally used in China to frighten away unsettled spirits or "Hungry Ghosts." These are believed to be the spirits of the deceased who have been buried without adequate funeral rites and continue to wander the earth. At New Year, they are frightened off with firecrackers, but at the Hungry Ghost festival, on the fifteenth day of the seventh lunar month, their spirits are appeased with offerings, prayers, and liturgies in the hope that they will be placated and respond benevolently.

Wind chimes have now gained a wider usage and are hung to help dispel negative forces as well as activate chi in an area where it may be slow-moving. They are also a useful indicator of someone entering a room in situations where your view of the door is obstructed.

Wind chimes activate slow-moving chi and dispel negative forces.

IMPROVING YOUR FENG SHUI

諧 Harmony

This part of the workbook takes you on a step-by-step journey through the rural landscape and into an urban environment, including readings for specific rooms in your home or workplace. The general principles and guidelines contained in each section are intended to help you understand the flow of chi in specific areas and determine why it may be disturbed or blocked. Suggestions to improve weak areas or encourage a more even circulation of chi are offered throughout.

PART

2

How to Use Part Two

Flow

In this part of the book, a wide range of examples are covered, from the pattern of roads around your home to the design of your house or apartment. We have looked at the most favorable positions for items of furniture, particularly couches, ovens, beds, and desks, and their siting in relation to doors and windows, and have suggested simple solutions. These are guidelines and not absolute rules. Every home and every person is different, and you may feel comfortable, relaxed, and protected without having to make any alterations. For example, if you are studying at home or working in an office, your back should have the support of a wall to help you concentrate, but you may find that sitting at a desk facing an open window enables you to focus on your work and increases your productivity.

On other occasions, you may feel something needs changing but are not sure where or how to begin. Our guidelines will help you understand how the shape or position of structures or furniture might exert an oppressive influence, or how open doors and windows may make you feel vulnerable or drained. Sometimes a minor alteration to your surroundings, such as clearing away clutter, hanging a blind, or introducing gentle lighting, can exert a subtle and positive change. The guidelines are there to help you, not disturb you, and you should follow what you feel is most appropriate to your circumstances.

Each section is highly visual, and the at-a-glance illustrations will help you to understand immediately whether the feng shui in each example is good or bad. The unique key system reinforces this instant interpretation; every illustration features a symbol that identifies whether the feng shui depicted is good, bad, or whether steps have been taken to remedy the situation, and thus the feng shui is improved (see page 49). You should refer to all the illustrations to determine which aspects of the examples shown are most applicable to your own surroundings.

Advice is given for all situations where the feng shui needs improving (in some instances the same advice applies to two or more illustrations). After you become familiar with the principles, you will begin to get a feel for an ideal feng shui site and apply this knowledge to your own surroundings.

Feng Shui Key to Illustrations

 Good feng shui

 Bad feng shui

 Improved feng shui

The Landscape

Feng shui literally means "wind/water." You can see the powerful shaping effects of these forces in the natural world. A cold, windswept site often has low, patchy vegetation so chi is quickly dispersed, whereas a landscape of gentle hills and rivers allows for greater plant growth and provides protection from the elements. In the rural section, a variety of landforms and river courses are illustrated, and the type of energy they create is also explored. On a wider level, there is the overall balance created by the hills, plains, or rivers, but there are also animal and elemental shapes and patterns in the land or on water, all of which have an effect on those living nearby.

Roads, Homes, and Offices

Many of the principles that apply to the flow of rivers also apply to the pattern of roads; similarly, the principles for a well-protected rural site also apply to an urban site. The range of examples given can be used whether you live in a small town or in the heart of a city. A variety of housing styles are covered, ranging from high-rise apartment buildings to detached houses.

The demands of the workplace are different to those of domestic needs, and so the business section stands on its own. Because businesses are usually reliant on clients or customers, they should be sited in busy areas where there is already flourishing business chi. They are also able to thrive on a greater degree of activity, traffic, and noise than would suit a normal household. You should, however, gauge the information according to the nature of your work. If your work is dependent upon a quiet environment, you may find that the section on the shape of buildings and layout of offices is more pertinent than the section on the site of a business.

Taking a Pa Tzu Reading

You can take a personal pa tzu reading (see page 37) for a complete floor plan of your home, office, or specific room. Sample readings have been included for the kitchen, living room, and main bedroom. You can choose to carry out a reading for any room in your home, but remember to align north on your pa tzu compass with the northern direction of the room. In the workplace, the position of desks is important, particularly the manager's or director's desk, so a sample reading is given for a small open-plan office.

The sample readings include suggestions for change according to the elemental combinations. If you feel the room already has a positive and smooth flow of chi, changes may not be necessary.

OUTSIDE
THE HOME

Chi is manifest in all natural phenomena. It is seen in towering peaks, steep cliffs, fertile land, rolling hills, open plains, and fast-flowing rivers. In each place, chi is different, sometimes dangerous, other times benevolent. For example, a site where stormy waters break against craggy cliffs is powerfully yin and the chi here can be overwhelming, but water spreading gently across fertile land is yang and the chi is life-giving. The ideal site combines even-flowing, active chi, both on land and in water, to create a balance between yin and yang; when the two are in harmony, they nourish and energize each other.

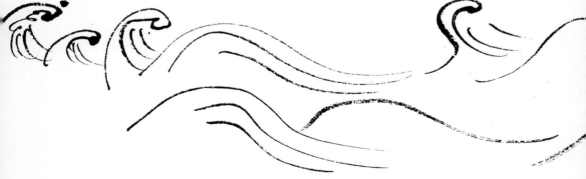

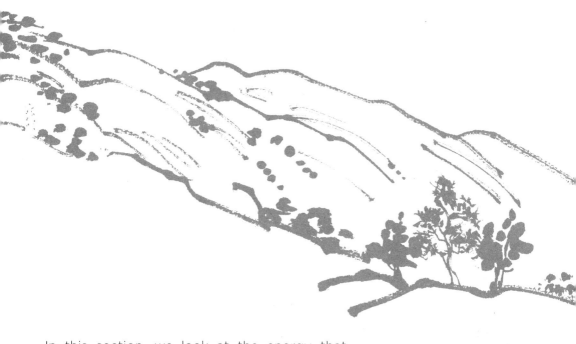

In this section, we look at the energy that is present in and around landforms and the influence it may have on that site. Examples are given of specific patterns and shapes that can be identified in the land, on water, and in roads (in both rural and urban situations), because the flow of roads follows many of the principles that apply to the flow of watercourses. There are, of course, hundreds of forms that can be read in the landscape by an experienced feng shui practitioner, but this brief section opens the way to seeing and understanding the landscape from a new perspective.

Mountains, Hills, and Rivers

While chi is present in all places to a greater or lesser extent, the actual shapes of the land, rivers, and sites where the land meets the sea are identified with elements, animals, birds, and other phenomena. Some are seen as guardians protecting the site, making it a safe and auspicious place, while others are ready to devour the site, bringing misfortune to those who live there. Some are passive and do not convey any particular influence on an area, and others are dynamic, producing powerful and effective energy.

This section shows you how to interpret these various shapes in the landscape and determine whether they have a positive or negative effect on your surroundings.

The Four Guardians

In feng shui, the traditional guardians of a site are the Green Dragon, Red Bird, Black Tortoise, and White Tiger, as we discovered earlier on page 22. These are the creatures that can be identified in the actual lie of the land around any site. They may be perfectly proportioned, bringing good fortune to the area, but sometimes the landforms associated with them are weak and, therefore, their protective power is diminished. When these four creatures are in harmony with one another, the site benefits from smooth and beneficial chi.

An ideal site for the animal spirits—they are balanced in the landscape, protecting the house in the center.

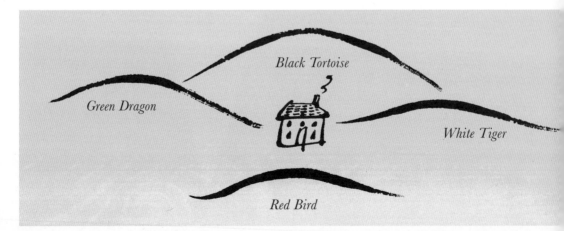

Black Tortoise

Green Dragon

White Tiger

Red Bird

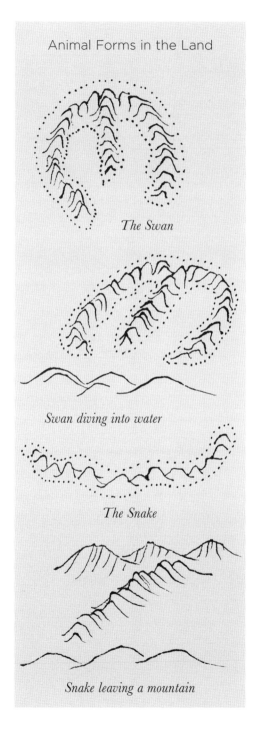

Animal Forms in the Land

The Swan

Swan diving into water

The Snake

Snake leaving a mountain

Animal Forms in the Land

Specific features in the land can bestow an energetic quality on the landscape. Sometimes a site has the basic shape of an animal, but it is not as powerful as a site that depicts the animal when it is in motion.

For example, when the shape of a Swan or a Snake appears in the landscape, it offers a positive reading (see illustrations left). The land will prove to be a good site on which a family can live for a generation, but it will not be able to sustain continual building by successive generations. When the animal is in motion, such as the Swan diving into water or the Snake leaving a mountain, the land is endowed with regenerative qualities that can sustain a variety of use. In addition to producing beneficial chi, these active landforms have the power to store and spread chi.

There is a wide variety of intricate animal formations that will be familiar to a skilled feng shui practitioner; however, it is still possible for any one of us to look carefully at the land and read its shapes. Certain formations take on a nourishing aspect: the hills may form wide, gently sweeping arms and the sites may nestle inside, resembling a dragon protecting a pearl. Other sites may have a more ominous energy; for example, the shape of jagged cliffs might look like tigers ready to pounce. The important rule is to stop and study the site, look at its shapes and forms, follow the basic guidelines, and see what kind of energy emanates from the area.

The Water Dragon

Just as animals can be seen in the contours of the land, they can also be identified in the contours of a river and the surface patterns created by the flow of water. While specific animals might be associated with certain shapes, the actual twists, branches, and bends of all rivers are known as the Water Dragon. The many formations that watercourses follow are given a feng shui interpretation in a Chinese text known as the Water Dragon Classic. Here, the ideal site nestles within the inner curves of a watercourse that is nourished by an outer, curved watercourse, thereby protecting the site in the "stomach of the dragon." Gently flowing water that follows a meandering course also creates nourishing chi, and sites located in these curves are embraced by the Water Dragon.

If the flow of water is hurried and turbulent, the site is drained of energy, while straight or sharply turning river-courses are like secret arrows cutting into the wealth and health of those living nearby. Such unfavorable sites need protection in the form of other buildings or natural features—raised land or vegetation, for instance. Examples of various sites are shown on the next page.

Coastal Waters and Lakes

Readings for coastal waters are taken from the patterns created by the wind, by its contact with the land, and by the channels of water that flow into the sea. Readings for lakes are also judged by the surface patterns as well as by the shape of the lake and the tributaries leading to it.

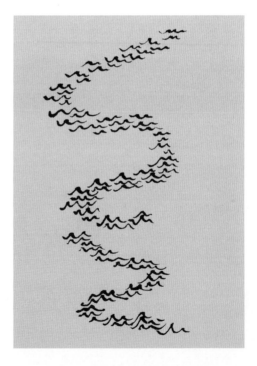

The pattern created by the wind on the surface of this water creates an animated and auspicious shape called Submerged Dragon Swirls Tail.

As with the land formations, there is an extensive set of patterns that can be identified in a body of water by an experienced feng shui practitioner. For the less experienced, the key to understanding water formations is to look for water with an even flow or a regular pattern so that the chi created not only nourishes the land but also enriches those living in the vicinity. Sluggish, stagnant, or polluted water is a source of sha (destructive vapors), while rapid-flowing or rough water can quickly disperse chi.

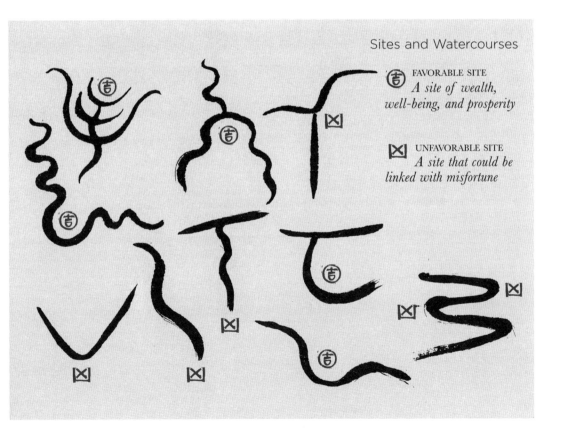

Sites and Watercourses

FAVORABLE SITE
A site of wealth, well-being, and prosperity

UNFAVORABLE SITE
A site that could be linked with misfortune

The Five Elements

The five elements of wood, fire, earth, metal, and water can be seen in specific shapes in the land, rivers, and streams. Sometimes the elements are repeated in a certain sequence or they combine to produce sites that possess powerful and productive chi (see example below). When you are familiar with the relationship between the elements, you should be able to identify the elemental shapes in the landscape and determine whether they are harmonious or whether the patterns they form are negative.

Land

Many land formations are traditionally used as examples of identifying combinations of elements in the land—some have even been attributed with symbolic names.

In the landscape illustrated at the bottom of this page, the range of hills shaped like the water element nourishes the wood-shape hill, and together they meet earth, which gives them a solid grounding. This produces a range of mountains known as Roots Digging Deep into Firm Foundations.

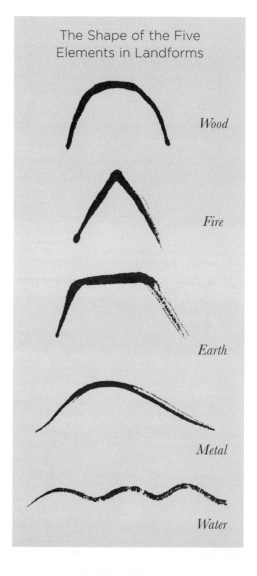

The Shape of the Five Elements in Landforms

Wood

Fire

Earth

Metal

Water

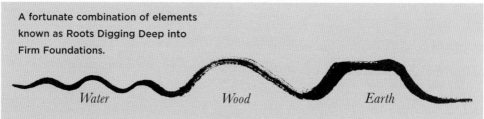

A fortunate combination of elements known as Roots Digging Deep into Firm Foundations.

Water   *Wood*   *Earth*

The formation of this site is said to grant prosperity and wealth.

Water

According to the Water Dragon Classic, the elements of water, earth, and metal are the luckiest combinations, because their shapes are softer and more gentle, thereby encouraging the even and productive flow of chi.

When different river shapes combine, they can create beneficial or unlucky feng shui, depending once again on whether these elements have a creative or destructive relationship. For example, a water-shape river entering a metal-shape river is a positive combination, and a site here will probably receive its beneficial influence, whereas a fire-shape river entering a metal-shape river could exert a malign influence on the site, because fire destroys metal.

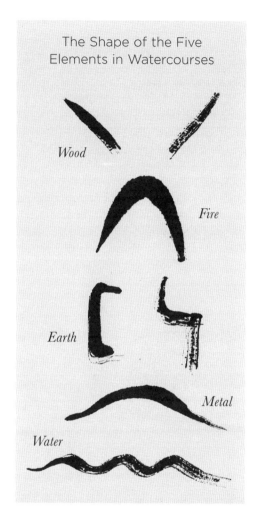

The Shape of the Five Elements in Watercourses

Wood

Fire

Earth

Metal

Water

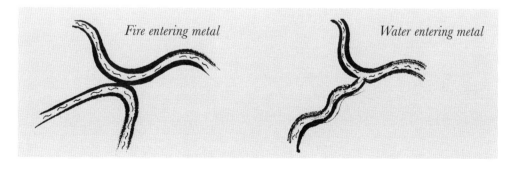

Fire entering metal

Water entering metal

Feng Shui in Rural Landscapes

If you live in a rural landscape, you are close to the deep energy that exists in landforms and can include local and distant features in your reading. One of the most important factors to consider is the level of protection offered by the natural environment. Ideally, the four guardians should be seen in raised land behind and on each side of your house. The land should not be scarred or devoid of vegetation, because this saps the earth's energy. The height, shape, and proportion of raised features also need to be observed, because these can overshadow your home or create narrow wind tunnels or a downward rush of chi.

Houses that are isolated and open to the elements are also vulnerable. In the absence of natural protective features, build a screen of trees or erect other buildings to act as a defense against adverse weather and the uncontrolled flow of chi.

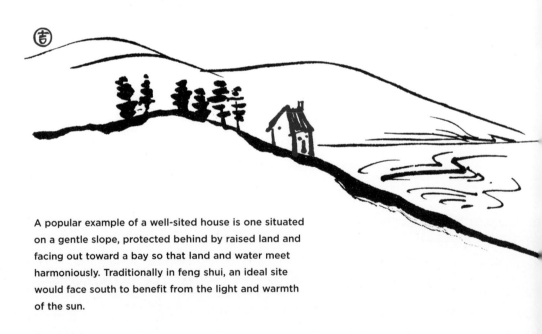

A popular example of a well-sited house is one situated on a gentle slope, protected behind by raised land and facing out toward a bay so that land and water meet harmoniously. Traditionally in feng shui, an ideal site would face south to benefit from the light and warmth of the sun.

 Good feng shui   Bad feng shui   Improved feng shui

A house perched on the top of a hill or cliff is too isolated and chi is quickly dispersed. It is like a lonely guard on a hill and needs other buildings, fences, or trees to provide protection.

BELOW If the hill behind the house is too steep, the beneficial chi rolls straight past the house, and as a result, the occupants may find that good fortune quickly slips away. These houses need support, both at the back and the front, to curb the fast flow of chi.

ABOVE An overhanging cliff is oppressive for those living underneath, because its weight presses down like a lid. Pointed objects could be placed on the roof of the house to resemble chisels cutting into and weakening the weight of the rock.

The front of the house should not be enclosed by clumps of trees, which have powerful yang energy and also prevent light from entering the house. The height and density of the trees should be kept under control and the occupant should be alert to the possibility of the trees' roots undermining the foundations of the building.

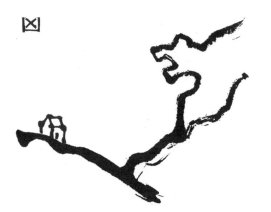

LEFT This house faces a cliff that resembles a tiger ready to pounce. Certain shapes in the land can bestow positive energy, because they resemble auspicious features, such as a book or pen indicating scholarly success, but this crouched tiger is potentially dangerous. Install a mirror to reflect the tiger's image and place a hunting weapon (or a replica of one, for safety considerations) in the direction of the rock.

 Good feng shui   Bad feng shui   Improved feng shui

The hillside near this house has a smooth indent resembling a large rice bowl, which could be seen as a sign of a regular food supply and, therefore, prosperity. The land in front also gently rises, so the house is not overpowered by the gradient of the hill.

The current from electric pylons close to a row of houses could throw chi into disarray and affect the health and relationships of those living there. Their impact can be reflected back or absorbed by a large tray or container of absorbent material, such as wood chips or sand.

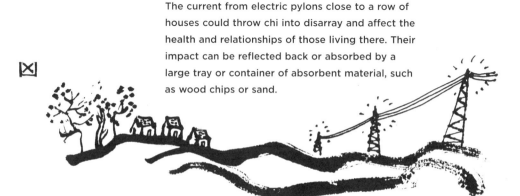

These houses are set in a wide, gently undulating valley, protected by a higher range of hills to the back and slightly lower ones to the side and front, echoing the ideal four-guardian formation. A site such as this is conducive to an efficient and smooth flow of chi.

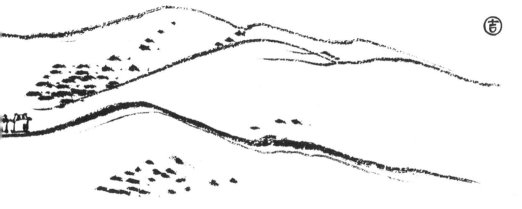

Chi is oppressed and trapped by the steep hills and narrow valley floor. The amount of light entering is limited, and the valley could act as a windtunnel, funneling chi and negative forces rapidly through this space. Although the landform cannot be altered, the occupants should try to shield the immediate area around their houses from this rapid flow. Trees or terracing on the hillside would also help to control chi running quickly down these slopes.

The hills around these houses are dotted with shrubs and stunted bushes, giving the impression of scars or acne, which could affect the health of the nearby residents. Try to landscape the area around the houses with well-kept trees and flowers to produce life-giving chi and, if possible, incorporate round structures in your design.

This featureless landscape is dotted with low-lying sparse vegetation and is subject to strong winds, so chi passes swiftly and is soon dispersed. The house needs protection from outbuildings or trees to avoid it being the target for destructive energy.

Although these houses are built on flat land with few raised features, the trees and shrubs help to regulate the flow of chi and enable it to circulate smoothly. Other buildings, such as gazebos or small barns, would also help control energy flow.

Road Patterns

Roads are major channels along which chi circulates, and, therefore, they influence the energy in your home and local area. The flow of chi depends on the formation of the roads and their relationship with natural or man-made features. Roads are the urban equivalent of rivers in a rural landscape, so many of the rules that apply to watercourses also apply to roads.

The most beneficial chi is created by gently curved roads. Chi is concentrated at busy intersections or converging roads, is blocked in narrow, cramped conditions, and is funneled down straight, arrowlike roads. The flow of chi can quickly change if it is confronted by a sudden narrowing of a wide road, when it meets a series of sharp bends, or when it is abruptly trapped by a dead-end and its negative effects rebound on the nearby buildings. The condition of road surfaces also affects feng shui. Surfaces should be even and well-maintained; smooth dirt roads are the most beneficial, because they are directly in contact with the earth's energy.

The pattern and shape of roads also take on certain characteristics that influence the site. A gently curved road wraps itself around sites like a "jade belt," a V-shape road resembles a pair of scissors cutting into the site, an overpass can be likened to a scythe, while an even, winding road may resemble a dragon and thus bestow good fortune on that site.

A house or apartment on one of the corners of a crossroads is subject to the convergence of chi from several directions and the sharp corners accentuate destructive chi. The house is also affected by the movement of traffic from four directions, particularly when vehicles turning at the crossroads appear to be heading toward the front door. A mirror outside the house will help to deflect the influence of oncoming traffic, while blinds offer added protection.

 Good feng shui   Bad feng shui   Improved feng shui

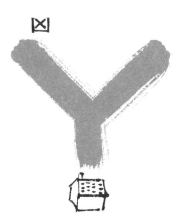

A house or apartment building built at the end of a long, straight road is subject to sha, because of the force of the energy being funneled down this direct, narrow route. (See advice on page 66.)

The Y-shape road causes confusion for the occupants of this building. They may find it hard to make important family or business decisions. (See advice on page 66.)

Destructive forces are focused at the sharp point where the road forms a V. The negative energy that accumulates at this point could affect the health and relationships of those living nearby. (See advice on page 66.)

The chi traveling down the road toward the T junction becomes too forceful as it meets the intersections and can affect the prosperity of those facing the junction or living at a point between the two junctions. Use reflective objects to protect the site and create a barrier with blinds, shrubs, or fencing.

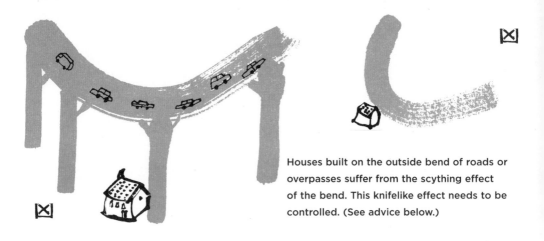

Houses built on the outside bend of roads or overpasses suffer from the scything effect of the bend. This knifelike effect needs to be controlled. (See advice below.)

Because there is only one narrow exit from these culs-de-sac, the energy is easily trapped. The residents may find that their finances and general good fortune are being squeezed out; the circular site *(left)* even resembles a noose. Additional small exits or paths would help to prevent energy from becoming trapped and decayed.

• *Advice* You can use a mirror or other reflective object to reflect back destructive energy; if you place a small sword or spear (or a model of one) above it, pointing toward the road, it will enhance the mirror's energy. It will also help the site if there is a curved path leading to the building to control the flow of chi as well as ease the effect of negative forces. You can screen the front door with a porch, and a row of bushes or small trees will give added protection.

 Good feng shui   Bad feng shui   Improved feng shui

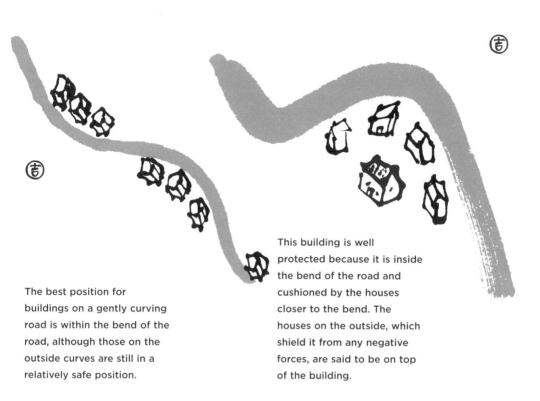

The best position for buildings on a gently curving road is within the bend of the road, although those on the outside curves are still in a relatively safe position.

This building is well protected because it is inside the bend of the road and cushioned by the houses closer to the bend. The houses on the outside, which shield it from any negative forces, are said to be on top of the building.

A complex pattern of roads with many twists and corners can confuse and trap the flow of chi. Try to create positive conditions in and around your house or apartment using greenery, rounded structures or designs, and appropriate light conditions.

Roads that converge near a bridge are a powerful meeting point for energy. While this busy site might be suitable for a store or restaurant, it can be overwhelming for a domestic residence, which would need to be well shielded by trees or a fence. You can use blinds or curtains as a barrier, and a mirror helps deflect forceful energy. The houses on the side road are better protected.

When roads branch off a main circular road, the homes that nestle within the inner branches receive the most beneficial chi.

Good feng shui   Bad feng shui   Improved feng shui

The buildings within the bends of a quiet road benefit from the gentle collection of chi, although the luckiest sites are those within the larger gap—the jade belt.

Although these houses are well-sited on this road, the good fortune normally associated with the site is reduced if there is a continual, heavy flow of traffic.

Many houses or apartment buildings are built along flat, straight roads, but this does not necessarily mean they have bad feng shui. The reading depends upon traffic flow, house structure, the amount of natural vegetation, and the surrounding features. Assess these aspects before deciding whether countermeasures are needed.

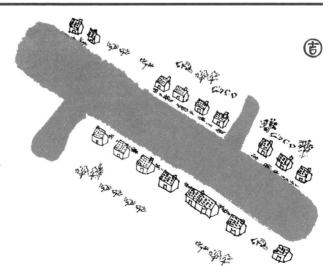

FEATURES AROUND THE HOME

When you are looking at a house or apartment, there are many factors that you automatically take into consideration. One will probably be its position in relation to other buildings—is it dwarfed by neighboring buildings, making it look dark or squashed? Perhaps it towers over its neighbors, providing a wonderful view but also making it isolated and vulnerable to the elements? You may also judge it according to its decorative appearance or structural design, and notice that the color of the bricks jars against the immediate environment, the window frames are rotting, or the front door is out of proportion to the rest of the house. These are all factors that are considered when assessing the feng shui of a building.

There are, however, many other points to take into account. Although less obvious, they could have a detrimental or enriching effect on the circulation of chi. These include the shape of the plot of land; for example, are there many curved or straight lines in the paths, borders, or features of the building, or are the sharp corners of other buildings or power lines pointing directly toward your home?

This section covers a wide variety of sites and conditions, working inward from the position of your house or apartment building in relation to other buildings through to assessing the access to the front door—the main path of chi into your home.

Houses in Relation to Other Buildings

The site of your home needs to be protected by neighboring features, but it also needs adequate space for energy to circulate. In built-up areas, structures surrounding your home represent the four animal guardians; in a semiurban area, the guardians can be seen in trees, neighboring houses, and landforms. Assess the angles and size of nearby structures for sharp corners or other features cutting into your fortune. Do taller buildings overshadow your home, or electric pylons and lines point in your direction? Some sites, such as playgrounds, convey positive energy, while a waste disposal site can be negative. Be aware of changing patterns around you, such as reflections from other buildings, fumes, and disruptive noise. You cannot usually change local features, but mirrors, vegetation, or screens can afford protection.

A house or apartment should not face a gap between two buildings, because the occupants' savings might slip through the narrow space. Move the main door so that it is not opposite the gap, or screen the door with a porch; in addition, you can shield the windows with shutters or blinds.

If the corner of a building faces the front of a house, it acts like a knife cutting into the owner's prosperity. A mirror would reflect back negative forces, but you can also shield the house with a row of trees, a fence (preferably covered in greenery), or with blinds on the windows facing the corner.

🏠 Good feng shui   ☒ Bad feng shui   🏮 Improved feng shui

Tall, thin buildings that tower over neighboring buildings are isolated and open to the elements. Chi is quickly dispersed and the upper part of the building is open to destructive energy. Individual apartments can be protected with mirrors, blinds, or curtains. Plants will also help to achieve chi.

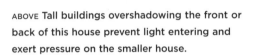

ABOVE Tall buildings overshadowing the front or back of this house prevent light entering and exert pressure on the smaller house.

ABOVE RIGHT The fortune of the middle house is squeezed by the weight of the taller houses.

• *Advice* Knife-shape objects or metal springs on the roof of the smaller building will act as a defense against the overpowering effect of the taller buildings (beware of bouncing destructive energy directly into a neighbor's house). If possible, greenery and water on the roof will also help to enliven chi.

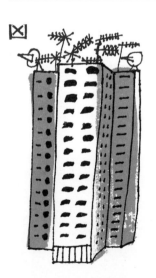

FAR LEFT Antennae, satellites, and masts are like weapons that cut through chi. Avoid living in or facing these buildings, but if you do not have a choice, you can absorb their impact with soft materials, such as sand, or send it back with reflective objects. If you are using mirrors, be sure that antennae or masts are completely reflected, so their destructive energy is sent straight back.

LEFT Small balconies on an apartment building do not disturb the overall balance of the building.

  Good feng shui   Bad feng shui   Improved feng shui

The houses alongside your house should be a similar height, those behind should be slightly higher to offer protection, while the land or features in front should be lower. This design conforms to the ideal positions for the four animal guardians surrounding a site.

A large building behind your house or apartment not only prevents light entering but acts as an oppressive force. You need to reflect or bounce this force away. Alternatively, you can cut into it with pointed, triangular shapes on your roof.

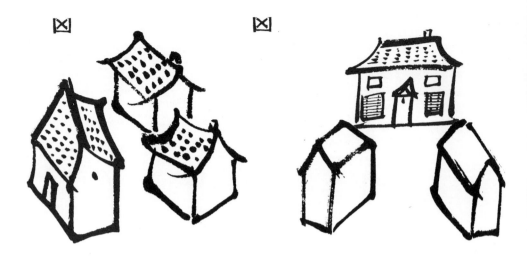

The roofs of houses located behind, to the side of, or in front of your house should not point toward your house as though they are piercing it. The pointed edges of sloping roofs, in particular, can cut into your home.

• *Advice* The cutting effect of roofs can be controlled by softening their impact with a tree or with greenery growing up the outside of your house. Blinds on the windows that are in line with the points of the roof facing your house will also have a shielding effect, as will a small mirror hanging on the wall or in the affected window.

 Good feng shui   Bad feng shui   Improved feng shui

Even if your house is well-positioned in relation to other houses, be aware of power lines, sharp corners, pointed features, and other subtle but negative forces that are directed at your home. The effect of satellites and antennae can be absorbed with sand or wood chips, or bounced back with springs. A pair of open scissors placed under power lines is also effective. Remove dead trees or vegetation close to your home, and try to create rounded edges to reduce the strength of negative forces and encourage a gentle flow of chi.

Many people do not mind overlooking a cemetery or a place associated with illness and death, but if you do feel uneasy or uncomfortable, put blinds on the windows or hang wind chimes over the door, which are believed to frighten away wandering spirits.

Places where the community gathers for prayer and meditation, or healing centers, often generate positive chi into the area. The same principle applies for schools, playgrounds, and day centers, because they are all places of activity, learning, and care.

Plots of Land

The plots of land shown below can be used for readings on detached houses, small rows of houses, and apartment buildings. There are two main considerations: first, the balance created by the building in relation to the surrounding land and, second, the ability of chi to circulate.

Chi is most beneficial when it flows smoothly over and around a site—thus curves and round edges create better conditions than sharp corners or straight lines. In a triangular plot, for example, destructive energy can settle within the sharp, angular corners. This can create unfavorable circumstances, because the house is contained within these points. If the land itself cannot be rounded off, create shields to block this energy, introduce objects to reflect it, or construct curved lines to enhance the flow of chi. A building also needs support and light. A lack of support can affect the stability and health of those living there. A lack of light creates a feeling of oppression and limits the beneficial effect of chi.

Rectangular or square plots of land are best, with a larger area at the back for protection in the Black Tortoise position. The land should slope gently from back to front. If the gradient is too steep with nothing to protect the house, chi rolls away, draining good fortune from the site.

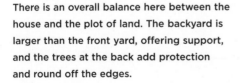

There is an overall balance here between the house and the plot of land. The backyard is larger than the front yard, offering support, and the trees at the back add protection and round off the edges.

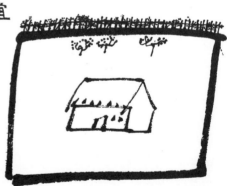

If there is a large, flat, and featureless area at the back, give the house some support by adding features, such as bushes, a rounded gazebo, small trees, or an ivy-covered fence.

If the backyard is small, do not overcrowd the space with trees, sheds, or a garage. Blinds or curtains on the back windows, or mirrors above the door, can give protection from overpowering features.

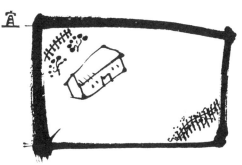

The back and front of this house face sharp corners, so round off the points with a screen, either an ivy-covered fence or bushes. You can use mirrors to deflect any malign influences that might accumulate in these corners.

Although this yard is relatively long, it is a positive layout, because the proportions are balanced. The house is given plenty of support at the back from the large yard, while the trees soften the edges and shield the house.

If there is a lack of space directly in front of the house, open land beyond the front yard will balance the site. If there is a road nearby, erect a small screen of bushes and curve the path leading to the front door to create the illusion of distance.

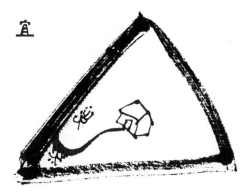

In a plot with sharp corners, the path to the house should not lead directly from a corner but instead curve gently toward the house. A pa kua mirror over the front door will help deflect any negative influences.

Adding to sharp corners or blocking them off with vegetation or garden structures, such as a greenhouse or shed, lessens the knifelike effect and eases the flow of chi around the house.

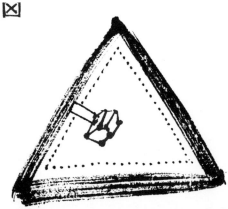

Soften the borders to create a curved effect, allowing for chi to flow more smoothly. Trees or fencing can be used as shields, but be careful they are not so large that they overpower the house.

Avoid laying out yards or paths with straight lines accentuating the angular shape, because these enable chi to move too quickly, and destructive energy will gather in the corners.

The curved borders enhance the flow of chi at the front. Although the shape is irregular, a balance is created, because the yard is in proportion to the size of the house.

The house faces a rounded edge, which is positive, and also has balanced space surrounding it, but it would help to strengthen the back corner with a border, shrubs, or a rounded gazebo.

Circular plots are good feng shui. There are no sharp corners to trap chi, and thus it is able to flow smoothly around the site, allowing for it to be at its most beneficial.

If the house is located on a small plot of land, it can use the land and buildings on neighboring plots to provide balance and support.

Assess the whole plot of a house or apartment building surrounded by buildings. Ideally, the buildings should echo the animal spirit formation (see page 23).

Yards

Vegetation provides life-giving chi and can enrich an area where chi may be slow-moving, dispersed, or trapped. But vegetation can also dispel chi or limit its effects; for example, a high, dense collection of trees can create excess yin, because of the dark, damp conditions around that site. Plants need to be used wisely to create balance and protection, encourage chi, and disperse sha.

When planning a yard, be sure trees or shrubs do not block your light or disturb the foundations of your house. Shrubs and trees can be useful for providing protection in a weak area as well as adding color and shape to your yard. Your garden plan may be relatively simple or it may be particularly complex. You might opt for a lawn surrounded by borders, or a yard that is broken into different sections. What is important is the cohesion and unity that it creates. Choose curved borders above straight or angular lines and use vegetation of different heights that blend well together. Always remember to clear away rotting vegetation or dead trees. If you are erecting a fence or a wall, grow plants up or close to it to gather more chi into the yard. Try to use garden furniture that is curved in shape or has rounded edges.

Round features or structures promote the smooth flow of chi. These include ponds, garden furniture, gazebos, and rounded edging on lawns. Pools of water and fountains are ideally located at the front of the house to attract distant good fortune to the area. Gentle activity in the water, either caused by aquatic life or by the breeze, increases life-giving energy. Pools and ponds should be cleaned regularly to prevent water from becoming stagnant and a source of destructive energy.

 Good feng shui   Bad feng shui   Improved feng shui

Do not let structures or features in the yard overwhelm the house or be out of proportion to the plot of land. If these features cannot be removed, use a mirror or a metal spring to deflect the pressure they place on the house. Adding greenery to outbuildings with climbing plants or small shrubs softens sharp edges.

If you live in an L-shape house, try to create a balance between the house and the open section by paving this area to create a patio or build a wooden deck. Lamps, wall lights, and container plants also help to activate chi in this area. The overall effect strengthens this open aspect and creates a symmetrical appearance.

Swimming pools have a strong yin nature that will overwhelm a house if too close to it; to avoid this, plant a screen of shrubs or build a low wall. The pool should be cleared of dead leaves or rotting vegetation to prevent sha settling over the pool and affecting the health of those using the pool or living in the house.

Taller trees and bushes positioned at the rear of the house will strengthen the Black Tortoise (although not planted too close to the house), and shorter shrubs and flowerbeds planted at the front will support the Red Bird.

If you have a small courtyard or balcony, introduce greenery, flowers, or climbing plants on the walls, because healthy plants produce life-giving energy. Do not, however, let trees overshadow the building, because they could exert pressure on the occupants.

The four guardian animals should be balanced in the yard just as they should be in the buildings around the house and the structure of the house itself. In the illustration (left), the density of trees on the White Tiger side

overpowers the flat, featureless lawn on the Green Dragon side. The height and size of the trees should be controlled and the Green Dragon should be strengthened with flowerbeds, shrubs, and trees (right).

Good feng shui   Bad feng shui   Improved feng shui

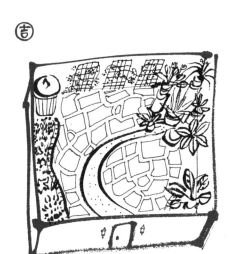

If you have a small, enclosed, paved yard behind your house or apartment, do not let garbage or other waste spread across this space. Keep the garbage covered and away from the back door of the building. The surface of the paved area should be smooth, even if the pattern of the paving blocks is irregular, and flowers or low shrubs should be planted in the available border space. Climbing plants trained up the walls will also help to soften the effect of brick or wooden fences surrounding the yard. Flowerpots are another means of introducing chi into this area—but keep the plants healthy, removing dead stems or flowers as necessary.

If you are creating a path through your yard, let it curve gently, and build up the vegetation gradually on each side. Put smaller, shorter plants close to the path and the taller ones at the back of the border. Choose colors and textures that work in harmony with each other to create a balanced and relaxing impression.

The Shape of Your Home

Balance, proportion, and protection are central factors when assessing the feng shui of your home. This section deals, in particular, with the shapes of buildings, whether they are single-family houses, attached row houses, or apartment buildings. There is no absolute set of rules, because a building can accommodate a wide variety of shapes, textures, and features and still maintain a sense of harmony.

Just as land is surrounded by four animal guardians, these guardians are also seen in the architecture of buildings. If several extra floors were built on the right-hand side of a building, the coordination between the White Tiger and the Green Dragon is disrupted, because the White Tiger becomes too powerful and may devour the Green Dragon (see page 87).

If one side of the house is taller or longer, it should be on the side of the Green Dragon, because this is a productive spirit. Do not, however, let it overwhelm the proportions of the building.

A building does not have to be perfectly symmetrical, however, it should be balanced—extra floors, additions, porches, terraces, patios, and unusual architectural features can all be incorporated into the design, but they should not overwhelm or weigh down one part of the building. Ideally, a house or apartment should have a greater depth than width to establish stability, although narrow buildings can gain support from the features surrounding the site.

Buildings should convey a sense of unity in their construction. If a building is disjointed, top-heavy, or confusing to look at, the occupants may also feel confused, tense, or under pressure. In contrast, a well-proportioned house encourages life-giving chi, thereby enhancing the well-being of the occupants as well as improving the feng shui of the immediate environment.

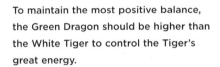

To maintain the most positive balance, the Green Dragon should be higher than the White Tiger to control the Tiger's great energy.

The White Tiger is a powerful and potentially destructive spirit if it dominates a building. Springs and mirrors on the lower roof help disperse its power.

The buildings shown here are all well-balanced shapes—the roofs and walls are in proportion to each other, creating a symmetry in the design. More unusual designs can also provide equally positive readings, as long as they create an overall impression of symmetry.

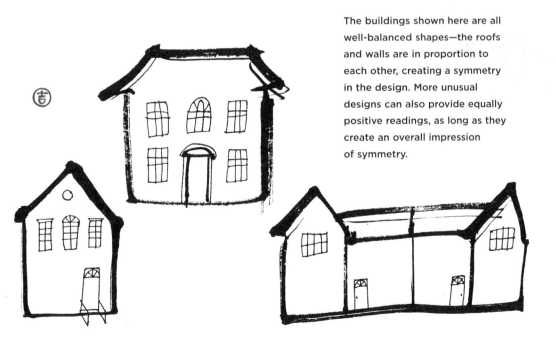

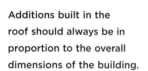

Additions built in the roof should always be in proportion to the overall dimensions of the building.

An addition should not overwhelm or overhang the house. You can place a spring on the floor to bounce away the pressure created by the overhang.

Small terraces or balconies will not disturb the overall harmony. A small awning can serve as a useful gathering place for chi but it should not extend too far.

Additions on the first floor add support to the house as long as they are not too large in relation to the main structure, but addtions on the floors above could make the house top-heavy.

Additions, sunrooms, conservatories, or features of the house with domed roofs encourage the even flow of chi, because their round shape is complete and, therefore, a sign of fullness.

Good feng shui   Bad feng shui   Improved feng shui

LEFT Small porticoed entrances or covered hallways do not disturb the balance, but porticoes that run the full length of a house could give the impression of a small fortress. This type of architectural device would, however, be acceptable for government or other public buildings.

RIGHT Small porches or additions to single-story buildings do not overwhelm the basic structure of the house. (If possible, try to incorporate rounded features in additions.)

Too many jagged features cut sharply through chi and can cause an unsettled atmosphere. Soften sharp angles with climbing plants or baskets; lights can also help to enliven chi.

A variety of sloping roofs and levels on a house could result in the occupants' profits rolling off. Rounded eaves or gutters will control this loss, and mirrors placed at the base of the slope will help to reflect it back.

LEFT If the size of the chimneys is out of proportion to the size of the house, they dominate the building and pierce the space above, making them subject to destructive forces.

BELOW A large house or apartment building can accommodate a variety of unusual or different shapes if each of the design elements is well-proportioned, thereby creating an overall harmony. While this range of windows, bays, and roof levels can sit easily on a larger house, do not cramp a small house with too great a variety of architectural detail.

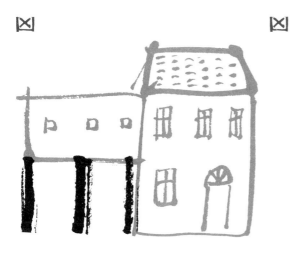

The support on the left-hand side of this building is hollow and weak and makes it appear as though half the house is sitting on stilts. If possible, this weak section should be walled in, creating a porch or atrium. The room will lack solid foundations, so it should be used for storage, not a bedroom or study.

When the garage is an integral part of the house, the car appears to be driving straight at the occupants. As the car moves into the house, it cuts through the chi and disperses its beneficial effect. Avoid using the room directly behind or above the garage as a kitchen, living room, or bedroom.

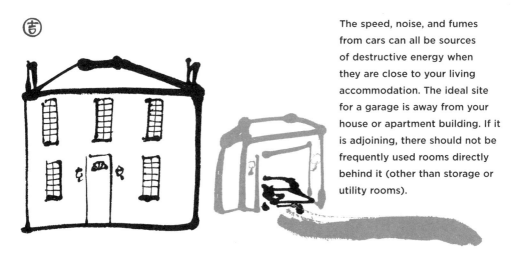

The speed, noise, and fumes from cars can all be sources of destructive energy when they are close to your living accommodation. The ideal site for a garage is away from your house or apartment building. If it is adjoining, there should not be frequently used rooms directly behind it (other than storage or utility rooms).

The Front Door

The front door is the main access for chi into your home, so if chi is blocked or trapped at this point, the occupants will not be able to benefit from its active and energizing qualities. Therefore, the main entrance to a building should not be enclosed on three sides or approached by narrow passageways. Similarly, the entrance to an apartment within an apartment building should not be in a cramped or poorly lit corridor.

If chi is funneled toward the front door down arrowlike paths, the impact on your home could be overwhelming. Paths that run steeply away from the front door result in good fortune rolling away from the house. It is important that chi is channeled evenly and freely toward the main entrance, while the door itself—the mouth of the house—should be well-maintained, upright, and in proportion to the building.

A downward slope sends chi forcefully toward the front door—the low dip is also a place where negative energy can collect. Terracing this area can help to regulate the flow of chi.

The access to the front door is open and the gently sloping backyard offers protection, because it strengthens the guardian spirit of the Black Tortoise at the back of the house.

ABOVE The access to the front door should be flat or sloping slightly upward so that chi can flow smoothly toward the front door.

RIGHT If the path leading to the front door slopes away from the house, a row of shrubs or small trees will help to slow chi running away from the site.

Chi can flow gently toward the house if the front path or driveway is evenly curved. Ideally, the driveway for a car should curve around toward the side of the house, and the path should lead from the driveway to the front door.

If the front door leads straight onto a busy main road, unpleasant traffic fumes and noise can adversely affect the health of the occupants. Shield the door or vulnerable windows with blinds or curtains, and activate chi with healthy plants, flowers, or shrubs. If the house is situated on a steep hill with the front door facing the road, erect a fence on each side of the house to control the flow of chi. The fence on the right blocks the onrush of energy; the fence on the left contains some of the energy as it sweeps down the hill.

A driveway that is wide in proportion to the size of the house funnels chi forcefully toward the front door. Dividing the drive into sections by placing shrubs or small trees at regular intervals will help to control chi's rapid approach. Lights on each side of the door will also help, as will an outdoor light on a lamppost, which will act as a guardian. Make sure that the lights are all working properly. Window blinds also help to shield the house from energy traveling down this wide path.

RIGHT If the path leading to your house is long and straight, its arrowlike effect can be lessened with a gate, a screen of shrubs, or a porch (particularly if the entrance is on the side). A pa kua mirror will also lessen the impact of negative energy.

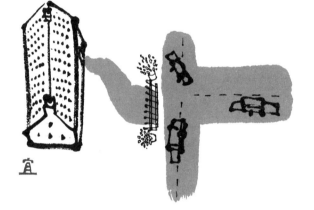

LEFT If a road points straight at your house like a knife, control the onward rush of chi and sha from it by creating a curved path leading to your house. A mirror above the front door will help, because reflective objects are particularly effective against oncoming traffic.

RIGHT Y-shape paths leading to the front door can cause confusion and indecision. Minimize the effect by blocking off one of the paths with shrubs; chi will then be channeled down one route.

FAR RIGHT A gap between two buildings directly facing a front door draws financial fortune away from the house—like a slice from a cake. Protect the front door with a barrier, but do not place trees or fencing too close to the house, or so high that they oppress those living there.

The front door should not be continually in the shadow of trees that obstruct the light and put pressure on those living inside. Cut any such trees back; however, there is no need to remove them completely, unless the roots are undermining the foundations.

Avoid planting large bushes or trees of the same size on each side of the front door, because they are said to resemble joss sticks (a type of incense stick) burning at each side of a grave. Make them different sizes or add more plants to one side to alter the effect.

Remove dead trees or decaying vegetation, and mend broken fences or sheds that are rotting. All of these items can be sources of destructive energy entering your home.

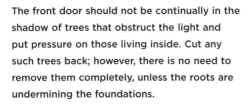

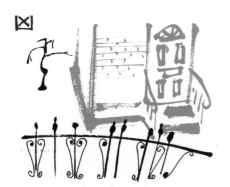

Do not place any garbage cans or containers of discarded waste near the front door, because sha accumulates here and will weaken the main access to the house or apartment.

LEFT A corner of another building directly facing your front door is like a knife slicing into the house. Try to screen your front door and reflect or bounce back the cutting effect of this corner.

RIGHT A pool of water in the front yard attracts positive chi, but if too close to the front door, it lets the strong yin nature of still water seep into the house. Water from a stream or fountain should flow toward the house; if not, it will carry away benevolent energy.

The front door, or porch around it, should not be out of proportion to the rest of the house. If the door is too large, the onrush of chi is too strong, making the house vulnerable to negative energy. In contrast, if the front door is too small in proportion to the size of the house, the access for enriching chi is limited.

A house with two main entrances is like a face with two mouths—the flow of chi is divided and the occupants cannot receive the full benefit, as they would from a single flow of energy. Do not use one of the entrances, and design the other door so that it is obvious which is the main access.

Make sure the front door is hung straight and that it is free of rot or damp. If the hinges and locks creak or squeal, oil them so the noise does not disturb the equilibrium of the home.

INSIDE THE HOME

Your health, relationships, and work can all be affected by the flow of chi through your home or by the buildup of negative forces in certain areas. The living room, dining room, and bedroom are traditionally regarded as the three most important rooms in the house, because you relax, eat, and sleep in these rooms. Nothing should be taken in isolation, however, and if the feng shui in these three rooms is ideal but the remaining rooms are overcrowded, dark, cramped, or poorly maintained, this will reverberate in other parts of your home.

When assessing your home, it is helpful to start by analyzing an overall floor plan using your pa tzu compass.

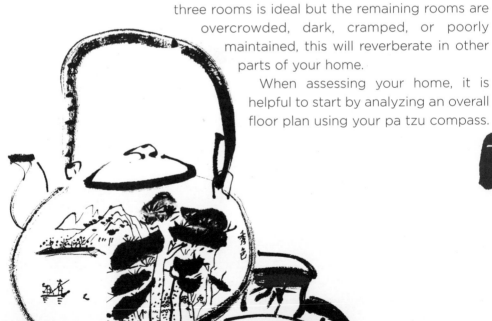

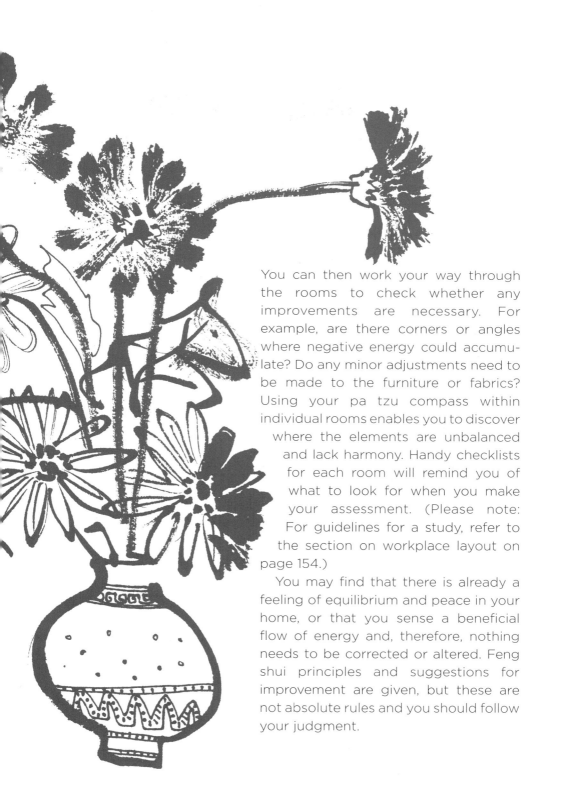

You can then work your way through the rooms to check whether any improvements are necessary. For example, are there corners or angles where negative energy could accumulate? Do any minor adjustments need to be made to the furniture or fabrics? Using your pa tzu compass within individual rooms enables you to discover where the elements are unbalanced and lack harmony. Handy checklists for each room will remind you of what to look for when you make your assessment. (Please note: For guidelines for a study, refer to the section on workplace layout on page 154.)

You may find that there is already a feeling of equilibrium and peace in your home, or that you sense a beneficial flow of energy and, therefore, nothing needs to be corrected or altered. Feng shui principles and suggestions for improvement are given, but these are not absolute rules and you should follow your judgment.

How to Analyze Your Apartment Floor Plan

Before you can carry out your reading, you need to know which of the eight pa tzu compasses belongs to your year of birth. You can learn the number of your compass, your lucky and unlucky directions, and your personal element by referring to pages 32–37.

We used pa tzu compass number 9 (see right) in the reading given below. The element for this compass is fire. Work through the example and apply the same technique to your own floor plan with your personal pa tzu compass.

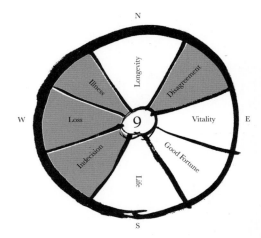

Pa tzu compass 9 • Element: Fire

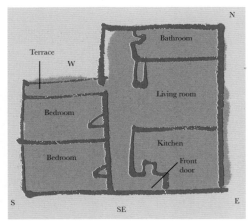

Scale drawing of apartment floor plan.

1 Overlaying your compass Draw a floor plan of your apartment (or each floor of your home) to scale and overlay your pa tzu compass, as explained on pages 36–37 (see opposite page also). Remember to align north on the compass with the northern direction of your apartment. Alternatively, use the compass printed in this book and stand in the center of your home, pointing north on your compass toward north in your apartment.

Your pa tzu compass is associated with only one element, but the eight directions of your apartment will each have their own element. Whether you are doing a reading of the floor plan of a room or house, these directions and their associated elements do not change.

BELOW **Directions and associated elements**

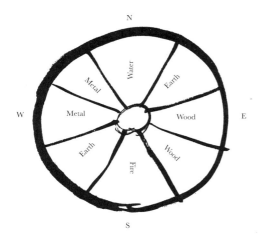

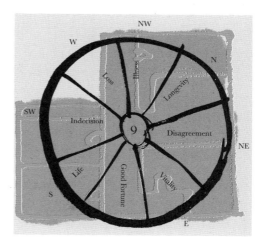

ABOVE **Overlaying your pa tzu compass on your floor plan**

3 **Working through unlucky directions** Work through each of your unlucky directions and its relationship with your personal element—in this case, fire—one step at a time.

BELOW **The unlucky directions and their associated elements**

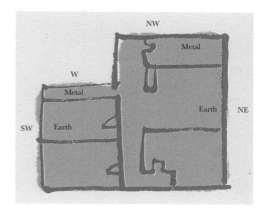

2 **Assessing the elements** You can see from our floor plan (above, right) that the four unlucky directions are in the northwest, west, southwest, and north-east, and these are the areas that need attention. Because the element that belongs to pa tzu compass number 9 is fire, you need to find fire's relationship with metal and earth—the elements associated with the four unlucky directions in this example (right). Look at the productive and destructive cycles of the elements shown on the next page.

☒ The northwest and west fall into the categories of Illness and Loss. The element associated with both these directions is metal. The table below shows that fire destroys metal.

This is a positive reading, because the powerful action of fire overcomes metal and improves the negative readings of these directions. Because fire is a powerful element, you do not need to strengthen it.

☒ The southwest and northeast fall into the categories of Indecision and Disagreement. The element associated with both these directions is earth. The table below shows that fire produces earth in the productive cycle.

This is an effective combination, because fire is in harmony with earth. If you want to strengthen the creative action of fire in the bedroom or living-room area, you can introduce various shades of red or orange into your color palette, as well as install additional lighting or hang paintings that depict fire. Do not, however, let the fire element become overwhelming. (See also pages 30–31.)

4 **Apartment layout** The entrance and the kitchen are both in favorable positions; the main route of chi into the home is through the front door, which falls into the Good Fortune section. The kitchen—which produces nourishment— is located in the Vitality section.

To be sure that chi can enter smoothly through the front door, check that the door is well-maintained and in proportion to the front aspect of the apartment.

You should also remember the position of the front door in relation to outside features, such as sharp corners, gaps, or dark or overcrowded areas. When chi enters the home, it will need space to establish its flow, so be sure there is adequate circulation to other rooms. In our apartment, chi has enough space, but it would be funneled into the house through a cramped, narrow corridor or if the doors to the bedroom and living room were close to the front door.

In this example, the bathroom is at the back of the apartment, away from the kitchen and with its doorway leading into the hall instead of directly into another room. It is in a strong position, because it is separate from the source of food and away from the living area. If there is only one door leading in and out of the apartment, however, there is a danger that germs could get trapped at the end of the hallway, making the chi sluggish and encouraging sha. Try to create an even circulation and keep this area free of clutter and waste; adequate lighting will also help to keep chi active.

Productive cycle	Destructive cycle
Wood produces fire	Wood destroys earth
Fire produces earth	Earth destroys water
Earth produces metal	Water destroys fire
Metal produces water	Fire destroys metal
Water produces wood	Metal destroys wood

The Hall and Stairs

After chi enters your home, it will need enough space to circulate freely so it can be evenly distributed throughout the rooms. If chi is blocked at this initial stage, its flow is disrupted and its beneficial effect weakened. Cramped or dark halls and stairways also encourage the accumulation of negative energy, which becomes trapped. Do not overcrowd halls or stairs with unnecessary furniture or objects, and if natural light cannot enter, make sure the area is well-lit and brightly decorated.

The front door should not open directly onto the stairs, because the rush of chi entering will be directed away from the first floor; this design could also provide a route for chi to roll out of the building. Chi needs space and light to adjust and circulate on first entering the house or apartment; beneficial conditions here also diminish the effect of negative forces that may be channeled or reflected toward your home.

If the front door opens directly onto a staircase, there is nothing to block or disperse negative energy entering the upper floors of the building. This design also enables chi to rush in, or flow down the stairs and travel straight out of the door. Do not leave the front door open, and create a screen with a large green-leafed plant or a piece of furniture. If, however, the house is small and the stairs are part of the living room, chi will be able to reach the first floor.

 Good feng shui   Bad feng shui   Improved feng shui

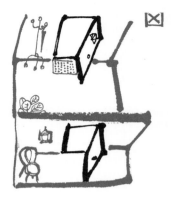

If the front door opens on to a dark, confined area, the circulation of chi into the main body of the house or apartment is cramped. Enliven the chi in this space with a healthy green-leaved plant, bright wall colors, and a mirror (but do not place the mirror directly opposite the front door). In dark hallways, keep a light on at all times.

The hallway or lobby is the main access for chi into the house or apartment, so keep the area clear of waste, crowded furniture, and sharp, angular objects. Create light, spacious conditions to encourage the efficient circulation of energy in the rest of the home. The activity of wind chimes above the door will also enliven chi in this space.

If the front door opens directly onto a door leading into another room, do not open both doors at the same time to prevent an overwhelming rush of chi into the house or apartment. For a small entrance space, such as the one shown above, keep it clean, clutter-free, and well-lit.

Avoid placing mirrors or knifelike ornaments directly opposite the front door, because they will reflect or cut through the incoming chi. (If you need to counteract negative forces here, use a small ornamental mirror.)

 Good feng shui   Bad feng shui   Improved feng shui

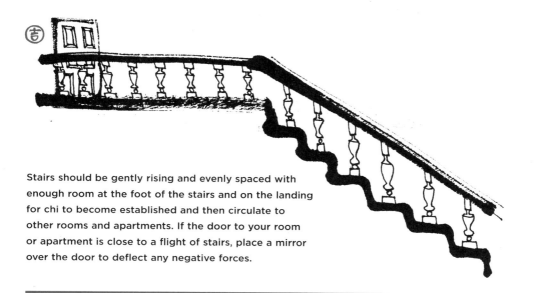

Stairs should be gently rising and evenly spaced with enough room at the foot of the stairs and on the landing for chi to become established and then circulate to other rooms and apartments. If the door to your room or apartment is close to a flight of stairs, place a mirror over the door to deflect any negative forces.

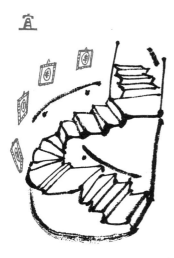

Chi can be channeled too forcefully up narrow, straight stairs or unevenly dispersed on winding, irregular stairs. If you cannot alter the layout of the stairs, make sure that the area is clean, brightly lit, and well decorated. Although you can use mirrors to deflect the flow of negative forces, do not hang one so that your head is cut off in the reflection. You can also use greenery, lamps, flowers, or pictures of landscapes to encourage beneficial energy.

Checklist

- Does the front door open into a bright, uncluttered space?
- Does the front door open directly in line with an inner door?
- Is there enough room in the hall or lobby for the smooth circulation of chi into the rest of the building?
- Is there adequate lighting in the hall or lobby?
- Is there a stairway close to the front door?
- Is the staircase cramped, narrow or poorly lit?
- Is there a landing at the top of the staircase?

The Living Room

The living room is usually the place where family and friends gather, so you need to create an environment that is conducive to relaxation and conversation. If the living room leads directly onto the street or if several doors lead into the room, it can leave you feeling vulnerable. In contrast, a dark, confined living area creates oppressive conditions.

Arrange your furniture to provide protection from the rush of energy that can enter through a doorway or large window, and do not face sharp corners or angular objects—they cut through beneficial energy. The couch is usually the item of furniture used most frequently; it, therefore, needs particular support from a wall or from another piece of furniture (the same principle applies for armchairs). As well as the seating arrangements, remember to take into account the height of the room—if the ceiling is too high in proportion to the size of the room, chi rises and disperses; however, if the ceiling is too low, chi is condensed and cramped. Do not put chairs under a beam; this could cause financial ruin or ill health. If the room is full of alcoves and corners, energy may be caught and trapped, so do not clutter these areas. In most cases, you can take appropriate measures to encourage a more efficient flow of chi through the use of color, lights, plants, reflective objects, blinds, screens, and furniture arrangement (see also pages 38–45).

Ideally, the front door should not lead straight into the living room. This is acceptable if the house or apartment is small, but if the living room is large, block the force of the incoming chi with a screen, bookcase, or partition.

If the kitchen and living room are open plan, try to screen off the kitchen area to prevent smells and steam from filling the area where you sit and relax. Clear away leftover food and empty the kitchen waste cans regularly.

The design of the living room should create an easy, relaxing atmosphere. Try to organize lights so they enhance it; do not use bright fluorescent tubes or bulbs directly above your head, because they may cause headaches and nausea. Avoid crowding the room with ornaments, sharp objects, and angular furniture— chi moves more freely around curved edges and symmetrical arrangements.

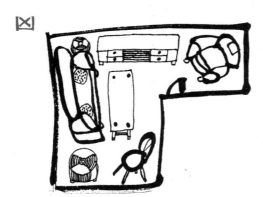

Do not create cramped passageways between furniture, because it funnels negative forces and limits the circulation of chi. If your living room is L shape, do not crowd the narrower part of the room with furniture or ornaments, and place lamps in dark corners.

Too much chi can escape through large windows or patio doors, particularly if they are opposite each other. Use blinds or curtains to control the loss of energy. The reading is, however, improved if the windows are divided into smaller panes of glass.

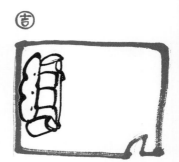

Avoid placing the couch directly opposite the door, because it will receive a rush of chi as the door opens and will be directly in the line of negative forces entering the room. The impact of chi can leave you feeling drained and vulnerable.

Do not leave yourself unprotected by placing the back of the couch directly in line with the door. If this arrangement is unavoidable, wind chimes over the door can alert you to someone entering the room.

Ideally, the couch should have the support of a wall behind it. This position lets you feel secure and in control, because you will be able to see who is entering or leaving the room.

 Good feng shui   Bad feng shui   Improved feng shui

If the couch is in the middle of the room, try to create some support behind you with a low bookcase, shelving unit, or screen.

A place where you pray or meditate should be distanced from noisy areas, open doors, or overhead beams. If space is limited, find a clean, peaceful corner in your living room where it is least likely you will be disturbed.

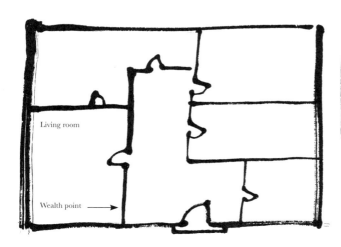

Living room

Wealth point

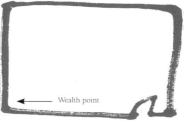

Wealth point

There is a part of the living room popularly known as the wealth point. It is said to be in the top left-hand corner, directly to your left instead of opposite as you enter the room. If there are two doors into the room, the wealth point relates to the door leading from the front of your home.

A doorway or arch in the wealth point creates a passageway for good financial fortune to slip through. Steam from a kettle, saucepan, or coffee maker at this point will also draw money away.

Checklist

- Is the couch (and/or armchairs) supported and protected?
- Are there doors opening in line with one another?
- Is there too little light in the room?
- Are there bright overhead lights?
- Is the flow of chi limited by cluttered furniture or ornaments?
- Are there many sharp corners or angular features?
- Do the windows need blinds for protection?
- Is there a lavatory door opening directly into the room?
- Is the couch positioned under a beam?
- Is there an eating area close to the area where you relax?

Keep any doors at the wealth point closed. Cover an archway with a screen or sliding doors. A plant with large, rounded, green leaves can enliven chi in this area. (Remember to remove any dead leaves or shoots.)

 Good feng shui   Bad feng shui   Improved feng shui

How to Analyze Your Living-Room Floor Plan

Before you can carry out your reading, you need to know which of the eight pa tzu compasses belongs to your year of birth. You can discover the number of your compass, your lucky and unlucky directions, and your personal element by referring to pages 32–35.

We have used pa tzu compass number 2 (see right) in the example given on the next page. The element for this compass is earth. Work through the example and then apply the same technique to your own living-room floor plan, using your personal pa tzu compass.

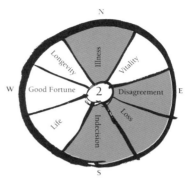

Pa tzu compass 2 • Element: Earth

ABOVE Scale drawing of living-room floor plan

1 Overlaying your compass Draw a floor plan of your living room to scale and overlay your pa tzu compass, as explained on pages 36–37 (see also left and page 112). Remember to align north on your compass with the northern direction of your living room. If you prefer, you can simply use the compass printed in this book and stand in the center of your living room, pointing north on your compass toward north in your living room.

Your pa tzu compass is associated with only one element, but the eight directions of your living room each have their own element. Whether you are doing a reading of the floor plan of a room or a house, these directions and their associated elements do not change.

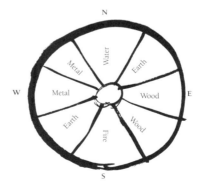

RIGHT **Directions and associated elements**

Overlaying your pa tzu compass on your floor plan

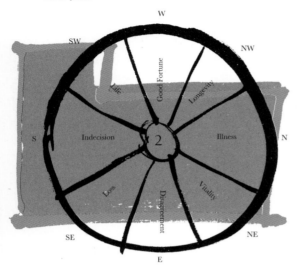

2 Assessing the elements You can see from our floor plan (above) that the four unlucky directions are in the south, southeast, east, and north, and these are the areas that need attention. Because the element that belongs to pa tzu compass 2 is earth, you need to find earth's relationship with fire, wood, and water—the elements associated with the four unlucky directions in this example (see floor plan on the right). Look at the productive and destructive cycles of the elements shown on the facing page.

3 Working through unlucky directions Work through each of your unlucky directions and its relationship with your personal element—in this case, earth—one step at a time.

☒ *South falls into the category of Indecision. The element associated with south is fire. The table below shows that fire produces earth.*

This is a good reading, because your element works in harmony with fire. The energy of fire is used to form earth, and in the process fire is drained as it nourishes and strengthens earth.

☒ *Southeast and east fall into the categories of Loss and Disagreement. The element associated with both these directions is wood. From the table we can see that wood destroys earth.*

Because your element is overpowered by wood, you have to find out which element weakens or drains wood. Wood produces fire, so the energy of wood is drained as it works to nourish and create fire. If you introduce the fire

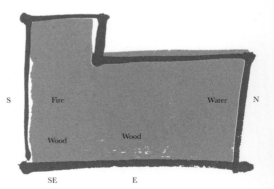

The unlucky directions and their associated elements

element through colors, textures, or fabrics, the power of wood will be channeled and weakened. You can use sources of heat, such as a real fire or an electric heater, objects, or paintings that depict fire, or warm colors with red or orange hues (see also pages 30–31).

The cycles of elements also show that wood is overcome by metal. When you use the destructive cycle, do not let one element attack another too forcefully. You could introduce metal ornaments, picture frames, or incorporate metal into furniture. Shades of white or cream can also be used effectively in fabrics, paintings, and color palettes. But do not overwhelm the room with one element, because it will disturb the overall balance.

[X] *North falls into the category of Illness. The element associated with north is water. From the table we can see that earth destroys water.*

In this combination, earth controls water and thereby strengthens the reading for this direction. You do not need to increase earth, because it is already strong. If you want to weaken the water element, channel it toward fire, because water is depleted as it destroys fire, and fire, in turn, strengthens earth. Do not overwhelm the area with fire, however, because you are working with the elements that overpower each other in the destructive cycle.

4 Room layout Examine the position of furniture and doors in your unlucky areas. In our example, the couch is in the Loss and Disagreement areas, but the back of the couch offers protection; when you sit here, you face Life, Good Fortune, and Longevity. The position of the couch is particularly important, because this is the place where household members talk and relax. Similarly, you can use armchairs to add support if their backs are to a wall in a weak area. The left and right doors open into Loss and Illness, but these areas can be strengthened using the elemental combinations described above. The table and chairs are in the Vitality area, so this is a positive place for eating, conversation, or study (keep the door closed to avoid being in the path of chi entering or leaving the room).

Productive cycle	Destructive cycle
Wood produces fire	Wood destroys earth
Fire produces earth	Earth destroys water
Earth produces metal	Water destroys fire
Metal produces water	Fire destroys metal
Water produces wood	Metal destroys wood

The Kitchen

For many people, the kitchen is more than a room to store and prepare food—it is also the place to meet, eat, play, and discuss ideas or difficulties. This is why the kitchen is regarded as a treasure; it is the place that nourishes the family. It also traditionally reflects the fortunes of the family, because the quality of the food indicates the family's prosperity.

If the house is compared to the human body, the kitchen is associated with the stomach—if the positioning and layout of the kitchen is harmonious, the health and well-being of the family will also be well-balanced.

In ancient China, the most auspicious site for a kitchen was the east, away from the south-facing front door and in line with the southeasterly winds that were useful for igniting fuel. In time, the south and the east became the traditional directions for a kitchen, because they also link in with the creative cycle of the five elements. Fire is the element associated with the south, and wood with the east; fire was needed to cook food and wood was the element needed to produce fire.

Today, kitchens are not orientated to any particular direction. However, it is important that the beneficial chi that may be present in this area does not quickly escape through doors that open in line with one another, or decay because of dark or unhygienic conditions. Because food is usually prepared using the oven, pay particular attention to its position, so that support and protection is provided for both the oven and the cook.

Ideally, the kitchen should have more than one door to prevent chi becoming trapped and drained as it circles around the enclosed space. Natural light, clear glass windows, ventilation fans, and other moving objects all help to encourage a more efficient and smooth flow of chi in, around, and out of the room. If your kitchen has no external window, effective ventilation and lighting will become even more important.

 Good feng shui   Bad feng shui   Improved feng shui

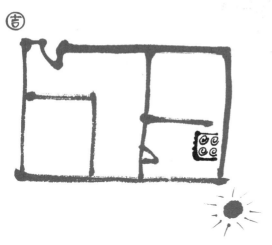

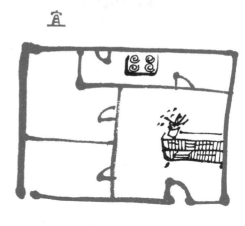

The south and southeastern sides of the house are traditionally the most favorable directions for a kitchen. Of more importance in modern kitchens are the circulation of chi, the arrangement of units and furniture, an adequate amount of light and ventilation, and a good level of hygiene.

The kitchen should not be directly in line with the front door. In addition to beneficial chi escaping, negative energy can travel directly to this important family room. You can form a barrier with a bookcase or unit of furniture, but if this is impossible, do not leave the front and kitchen doors open at the same time.

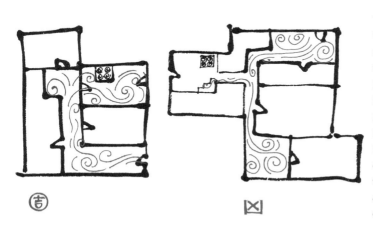

When chi is circulating through the house or apartment, it should be able to flow smoothly toward the kitchen (far left). If energy is hindered by twisting passageways and steps or long dark corridors, its flow is disrupted and its beneficial effect weakened (left). Keep these areas well-lit, and use a mirror to counteract the effect of sharp corners.

The entrance to the kitchen should not be directly in line with the back door of the house or apartment, because chi entering the kitchen could pass rapidly through. Try to divert its flow by placing furniture or kitchen units in this space. To prevent a forceful rush of energy, avoid leaving both doors open.

The kitchen should not be opposite or next to the lavatory, because germs and odors can spread into the area where food is prepared. If this arrangement is unavoidable, and the two rooms are close to each other, keep the lavatory door closed and keep the lavatory itself well-ventilated.

Do not block access to the kitchen with piles of papers, bags, or other household objects, which break the flow of chi. If the corridor leading to the kitchen is long and dark, decorate it with bright colors and use lights, greenery, landscape images, or pictures depicting peaceful activity to enliven chi.

Do not obstruct movement in the kitchen with too much furniture or with cluttered objects. The path of chi can be disrupted or trapped in crowded and untidy places. The kitchen should be a bright and healthy place, so avoid the buildup of garbage, piles of newspaper, unwashed laundry or dishes, and other obstacles that might inhibit the flow of chi. If the kitchen waste is not disposed of on a regular basis, sha enters and drains the life-giving energy that should be present in this room.

Good feng shui   Bad feng shui   Improved feng shui

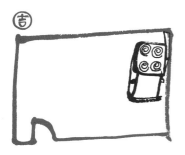

Position the oven so it is away from the direct line of the door. If you are standing at the oven with your back to the door, not only do you lack support but you will be unable to see who is entering or leaving. You can improve your sense of security by adding wind chimes above the door so you are aware of any movement there.

The oven should not be positioned under a window, because the food may deteriorate if exposed to sunlight. In addition, the oven itself lacks support in front. If you cannot move the oven, keep the blinds down or curtains partly drawn when you are cooking.

Do not leave knives or other sharp objects hanging from the units. In addition to being a potential health hazard, they also cut through the chi of the kitchen. When they are not in use, keep them in drawers or place them in a knife rack.

Avoid placing the oven next to the sink or the refrigerator, because the fire element of the oven will be overpowered by the water element present in these cold, wet areas. Place a panel, table, or saucepan storage unit between the two to create a barrier.

Checklist

- Is the kitchen directly in line with the front door of the house?
- Is the flow of chi to the kitchen hindered by dark or twisting corridors?
- Are knives or other sharp objects hanging from the kitchen units?
- Is the kitchen well-lit and well-ventilated?
- Is movement in the kitchen limited by furniture or clutter?
- Is the kitchen opposite or adjoining the lavatory?
- Is the oven positioned under a window?
- Can you see who is entering or leaving the room when you are using the oven?

How to Analyze Your Kitchen Floor Plan

Before you can carry out your reading, you need to know which of the eight pa tzu compasses belongs to your year of birth. You can learn the number of your compass, your lucky and unlucky directions, and your personal element by referring to pages 32–35.

We used pa tzu compass number 4 (see right) in the reading given below. The element for this compass is wood. Work through the example and then apply the same technique to your own kitchen floor plan, using your personal pa tzu compass.

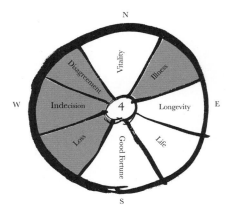

Pa tzu compass 4 • Element: Wood

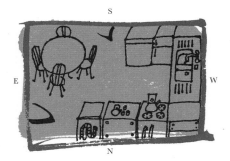

Scale drawing of kitchen floor plan

1 **Overlaying your compass** Draw a floor plan of your kitchen to scale and overlay your pa tzu compass, as explained on pages 36–37 (see above and right, below). Remember to align north on your compass with the northern direction of your kitchen. Alternatively, simply use the compass printed in this book and stand in the center of your kitchen, pointing north on the compass toward north in your kitchen.

Your pa tzu compass is associated with only one element, but the eight directions of your kitchen each have their own element. Whether you are doing a reading of the floor plan of a room or house, these directions and their associated elements do not change.

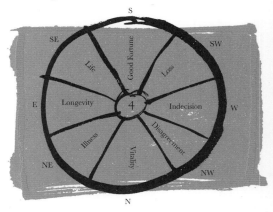

Overlaying your pa tzu compass on your floor plan

2 **Assessing the elements** You can see from our floor plan (see page 118) that the four unlucky directions are in the west, northwest, southwest, and northeast, and these are the areas that need attention. Because the element that belongs to pa tzu compass number 4 is wood, you need to find wood's relationship with earth and metal—the elements associated with the four unlucky directions in this example (see floor plan on the next page). Look at the productive and destructive cycles of the elements on the next page.

3 **Working through unlucky directions** Work through each of your unlucky directions and its relationship with your personal element—in this case, wood—one step at a time.

⊠ *West and northwest fall into the categories of Indecision and Disagreement. The element associated with these two directions is metal. From the table, on page 120, you can see that metal destroys wood.*

Your element is overpowered by metal, so you need to find out which element weakens or drains metal. Metal produces water, and as it works to nourish water its power is dissipated. As water gains strength, it then works to produce wood, which is your personal element. To strengthen water, introduce water colors or textures or water itself. Although black is the color linked to water, do not overpower the kitchen with black, but incorporate it through black cooking pots and pans, cooking utensils, or tones in curtains, blinds, or

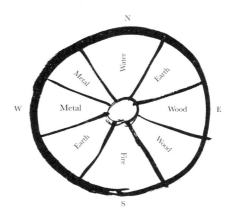

Directions and associated elements

flooring; these will all help to channel metal toward the water element. Water itself is usually already strong in kitchens because of sinks, washing machines, and refrigerators, so you may simply need to add a glass vase of flowers.

Metal is also dissolved when it has to work to destroy wood; therefore an increase in wood textures or colors will make metal work harder, and in this destructive process its power will be weakened.

If you look at the destructive cycle of elements, you will also see that metal is destroyed by fire. Fire is a powerful element by nature and, therefore, you should use it carefully. Because this reading is for a kitchen, the fire element should be present in a gas or electric oven, so you probably will not need to strengthen it.

⊠ *Southwest and northeast fall into the categories of Loss and Illness. The element associated with both of these directions is earth. From*

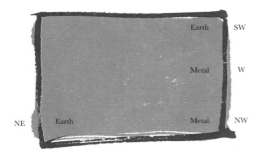

The unlucky directions and their associated elements.

the table below you can see that wood destroys earth.

Your personal element is already powerful and overwhelms earth, so you do not need to increase wood colors or textures in these areas.

4 Room layout The eating area in the east of this kitchen has a strong reading, because it falls into the categories of Life and Longevity. Anyone sitting at the table is also able to see who is entering through the back door, which provides a sense of security. One of the chairs, however, has its back to the inside door, so if you are sitting here, keep this door closed for protection. If you are eating or working alone at this kitchen table, the chairs with the strongest support are those with their backs to the wall.

The west side of the kitchen has the weakest readings, but these can be strengthened through the elemental combinations above. The reading is helped by the fact that the oven has the support of a wall in front and is not positioned next to the sink and refrigerator. Although you are working to improve the water element in this reading, the powerful water element present in the sink and refrigerator should not overwhelm the fire of the oven.

Productive cycle	Destructive cycle
Wood produces fire	Wood destroys earth
Fire produces earth	Earth destroys water
Earth produces metal	Water destroys fire
Metal produces water	Fire destroys metal
Water produces wood	Metal destroys wood

The Bedroom

Rest and relaxation are vital for your general health, and the quality of sleep you attain affects the harmony of the house and relationships between the occupants. This is why the feng shui of bedrooms is important. The main bedroom has particular significance, because the occupants who usually sleep here are the main source of the household income.

Although the design of the room and the features within it all need consideration, the position of the bed is most important. You are at your most vulnerable when you are asleep, which is why the bed should be protected. If the bed is positioned behind the door, you have no control over who is leaving or entering; if you sleep under a large window, the chi entering or leaving the room may be too powerful; if you sleep under beams or at a place where the roof rises to a point, you could be subject to headaches, nervous disorders, or general lack of energy. If the bed is in an alcove or there are shelves directly above the head of the bed, you may feel under pressure or claustrophobic.

Ideally, the head of the bed needs support from a wall and should be away from the direct line of the door. Avoid creating cramped or oppressive conditions by cluttering the room with furniture, ornaments, books, papers, or full wastebaskets. The use of light, textures, and colors in this room should also contribute to creating a tranquil environment, so you gain maximum benefit from the circulation of chi.

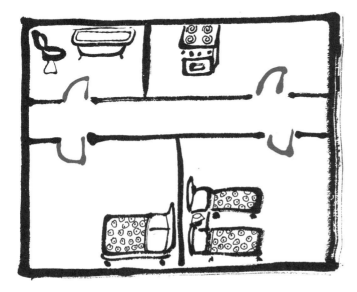

If the bedroom is opposite or connected to the kitchen or bathroom, keep the doors closed to avoid steam, smells, or germs spreading into the bedroom.

If the door opens onto your bed, your energy could be drained; a chest of drawers can act as a barrier.

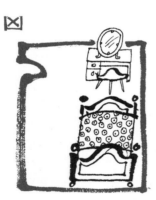

Do not hang or place a mirror directly opposite the foot of the bed, because you may be shocked if you wake up unexpectedly in the night and see your reflection.

For comfortable and secure sleep, the bed head needs support and protection. If the bed is in an open space, support the head with a small screen or item of furniture, but do not put heavy objects on it or let it jut out over the bed.

If the head of the bed is behind the door, you have no control over who is entering the room. This leaves you in a vulnerable position. Placing wind chimes above the door will help to increase your sense of security.

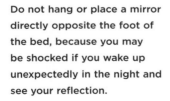 Good feng shui   Bad feng shui   Improved feng shui

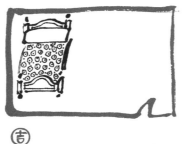

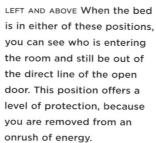

LEFT AND ABOVE **When the bed is in either of these positions, you can see who is entering the room and still be out of the direct line of the open door. This position offers a level of protection, because you are removed from an onrush of energy.**

Do not place bright lights over the head of the bed, because they disturb the equilibrium of the room and are said to cause eyesight or liver problems. Use soft colors and gentle lighting to create a feeling of tranquillity.

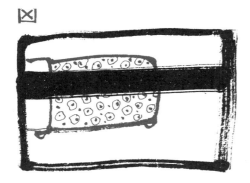

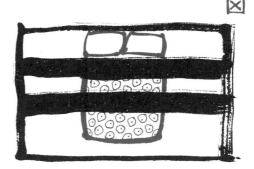

Exposed beams and rafters carry the weight of the house and put pressure on anyone sleeping directly underneath them. A beam that runs the length of the bed may cause headaches or nervous disorders. The beam could be covered by a false ceiling or you could hang a small reflective object from the beam to help disperse this pressure.

An exposed beam running across the middle of the bed is said to cause stomach disorders, while a beam crossing the foot of the bed could result in swelling of the feet. Reflective objects will help to disperse this pressure, or small springs under the beam will help to bounce it back.

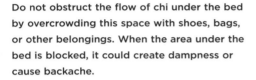

Do not obstruct the flow of chi under the bed by overcrowding this space with shoes, bags, or other belongings. When the area under the bed is blocked, it could create dampness or cause backache.

Do not place the bed directly under a ceiling fan or large light fitting, because it creates the feeling that the large objects are about to fall on the person sleeping below, resulting in disturbed sleep.

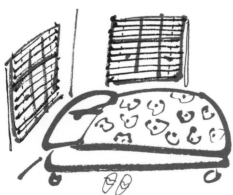

Avoid placing the bed directly under or beside a large window—not only is there a lack of protection but the amount of chi coming through the windows may disturb your sleep. If the bed cannot be moved, keep the blinds or curtains closed while you are resting.

Do not place a mirror directly opposite the bedroom window. The beneficial effects of chi are maximized when it circulates freely and smoothly, but a large mirror opposite the window will forcefully reflect back the incoming chi.

Good feng shui   Bad feng shui   Improved feng shui

Windows with one pane of glass should not be larger than the door. When the powerful chi coming from the window is combined with the chi coming from the door, the total effect can be overwhelming. Window blinds or half-closed curtains help to reduce this impact. (If windows are divided into smaller panes of glass, the flow of chi is diffused.)

Checklist

- Is there direct access to the bathroom or kitchen from the bedroom?
- Is the entrance to the bedroom clear of clutter and furniture?
- Is the bed positioned out of the direct line of the door?
- Is there support behind the head of the bed?
- Is the bed positioned under a window?
- Is there a beam running across the foot of the bed or over the top of the bed?
- Is there a bright light or bookcase over the head of the bed?
- Is there a mirror opposite the foot of the bed?

How to Analyze Your Bedroom Floor Plan

Before you can carry out your reading, you need to know which of the eight pa tzu compasses belongs to your year of birth. You can learn the number of your compass, your lucky and unlucky directions, and your personal element by referring to pages 32–35.

We used pa tzu compass number 7 (see right) in the reading given below. The element for this compass is metal. Work through the example and then apply the same technique to your own bedroom floor plan, using your personal pa tzu compass.

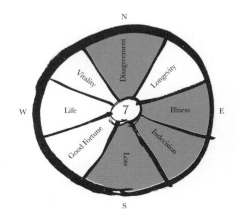

Pa tzu compass 7 • Element: Metal

Scale drawing of bedroom floor plan

1 Overlaying your compass Draw a floor plan of your bedroom to scale and overlay your pa tzu compass, as explained on pages 36–37 (see also above and page 127). Remember to align north on your compass with the northern direction of your bedroom.

Or you can simply use the compass printed in this book and stand in the center of your bedroom, pointing north on the compass toward north in your bedroom.

Directions and associated elements

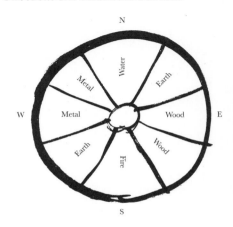

Your pa tzu compass is associated with only one element, but the eight directions of your bedroom each have their own element. Whether you are doing a reading of the floor plan of a room or house, these directions and their associated elements do not change.

2 Assessing the elements You can see from our floor plan (below) that the four unlucky directions are in the east, south-east, south and north, and these are the areas that need attention. Since the element that belongs to Pa Tzu compass number 7 is metal, you need to find metal's relationship with wood, fire and water—the elements associated with the four unlucky directions in this example (see floor plan on next page). Look at the productive and destructive cycles of the elements shown on the next page.

3 Working through unlucky directions Work through each of your unlucky directions and its relationship with your personal element—in this case, metal—one step at a time.

☒ *East and southeast fall into the categories of Indecision and Illness. The element associated with both of these directions is wood. The table on the next page shows that metal destroys wood.*

In this reading, your personal element controls the power of wood and you do not need to strengthen it further.

☒ *South falls into the category of Loss. The element associated with south is fire. The table on the next page shows that fire destroys metal.*

Fire is strong in this combination and, therefore, needs to be controlled or dissolved to weaken its destructive qualities. By introducing more of your personal element, metal, through metal

Overlaying your pa tzu compass on your floor plan

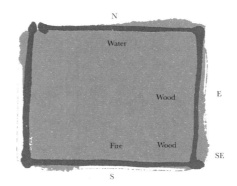

The unlucky directions and their associated elements

ornaments and frames, or tones of white, you can make fire work harder and thereby weaken itself (do not make the room completely white, because this resembles a hospital, representing ill health). Fire can be dissipated by making it produce earth, so if you introduce yellow hues or flowers into the room, fire's energy can be focused toward earth. Alternatively, because water destroys fire, tones of black can be used in fabrics, picture frames, or ornaments, or scenes of gently flowing water can be depicted in drawings or photographs. (See also pages 30–31.)

[X] *North falls into the category of Disagreement. The element associated with north is water. The table below shows that metal produces water.*

Your personal element works creatively with water, and although you can increase metal's effectiveness through metal ornaments, clocks, or tones of white, you do not need to make it too powerful.

4 Room layout The position of the bed is the most important aspect of any bedroom: sleep and relaxation are vital to physical and emotional health. In this example, the bed has a positive reading because it falls into the categories of Good Fortune, Life, and Vitality. The bed should be in a position that enables you to see who is entering or leaving the room; behind the door it is vulnerable, and directly opposite the door it is subject to the force of incoming energy. There is a light covered by a lampshade beside the bed; if this was a bare bulb, the glare could be harsh and disruptive. Lights above the head of the bed should be avoided, because bright lights can cause headaches or their effects result in disturbed sleep. The weak areas on the right-hand side of the room can be improved through the elemental combinations mentioned previously, but it is important not to disturb the flow of chi entering the room by hanging a mirror at the end of the wardrobe directly in line with the door or on the front of the wardrobe opposite the foot of the bed. The space in front of the door is left clear so chi entering the room can flow evenly and circulate freely.

Productive cycle	Destructive cycle
Wood produces fire	Wood destroys earth
Fire produces earth	Earth destroys water
Earth produces metal	Water destroys fire
Metal produces water	Fire destroys metal
Water produces wood	Metal destroys wood

The Bathroom

The bathroom and lavatory are a source of germs, and the sha that accumulates here could spread into the areas where you eat, rest, or sleep. Adequate ventilation is important to prevent the buildup of negative energy. Although the bathroom can be positioned on any side of the house, the door should not open directly onto the kitchen, bedroom, or living room. If at all possible, the bathroom should definitely not be sited at the center of the house or apartment, because germs could easily circulate to all parts of the house.

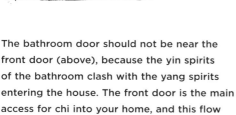

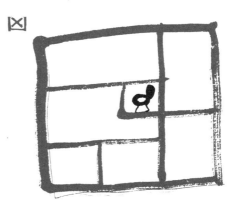

The bathroom door should not be near the front door (above), because the yin spirits of the bathroom clash with the yang spirits entering the house. The front door is the main access for chi into your home, and this flow could be disrupted by malign energy from the bathroom. Keep the bathroom door shut, particularly when the front door is open. Try to create positive feng shui conditions in the hall. If the bathroom is at the center of the home (above), there is a risk that sha will easily travel to all the surrounding rooms.

If you have a bathroom door that opens onto the kitchen, bedroom, or living room (right), it is important to keep the door closed to prevent the spread of sha.

The bathroom door should not open directly onto the lavatory or bath, because these are the places where you need privacy and protection (above left). If it does, and if there is enough room in your bathroom, position a screen or panel in the space between the door and the lavatory (above right). Avoid placing a mirror opposite the door, because incoming chi will be directly reflected back.

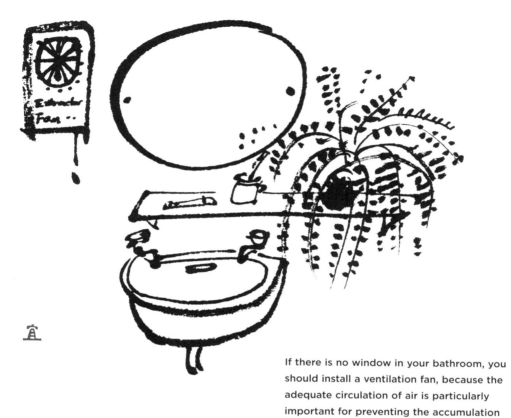

If there is no window in your bathroom, you should install a ventilation fan, because the adequate circulation of air is particularly important for preventing the accumulation of negative energy.

Checklist

- If there is no window, is there adequate ventilation and light in the bathroom?
- Is there any waste blocking the sink or are there wastebaskets left unemptied?
- Is the lavatory close to the front door, and if so, is the door kept shut?

- Does the lavatory door open directly onto the bedroom, kitchen, or living room?
- Are there blinds, curtains, or a screen to give you adequate privacy if needed?

The Dining Room

The dining room is a place for the family to relax, share conversation, and entertain, but, more importantly, it is a room where food is consumed and where family decisions might be made. For these reasons, it should not be too dark, cramped, or unprotected. Sometimes this room is also used as a study or work area, because the dining table is a useful place to spread out papers and books. In both cases, the dining room should not be subject to disturbing influences, such as traffic noise or doors opening and closing, thereby disrupting the room's equilibrium.

If there are doors leading in and out of the dining room, try to keep them closed when you are eating so you are not vulnerable to the flow of energy coming in one door and out of the other. This arrangement can make you feel nervous, hurried, or unsettled.

If the table is close to patio doors or a window with large glass panes, the food could be spoiled by sun or you may be subject to too much yin from cold or damp seeping into the room. Blinds or partly closed curtains will help to control these negative effects.

 Good feng shui   Bad feng shui   Improved feng shui

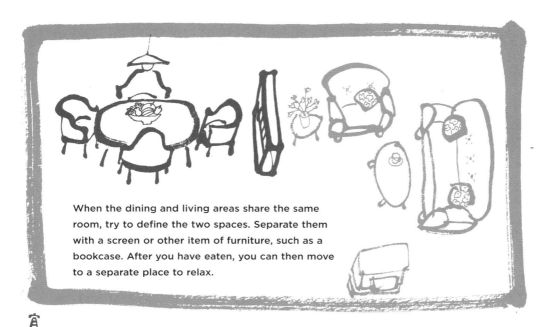

When the dining and living areas share the same room, try to define the two spaces. Separate them with a screen or other item of furniture, such as a bookcase. After you have eaten, you can then move to a separate place to relax.

If you are using the dining room as a study area, choose a seat with a wall behind it. This will give you protection and also help you concentrate. There is added security if you are sitting in a position from which you can see who is entering or leaving the room.

Checklist

- Is the eating area separate from the area where you relax?
- Are there two doors in the dining room directly in line with each other?
- Is the dining table close to a large single pane or patio window?
- Is there direct access to a bathroom or lavatory from the dining room?
- Is there adequate lighting in the room?
- Is there a clear path between the kitchen and the dining room so that hot plates and bowls can be safely carried?

IN THE WORKPLACE

The principles for feng shui in the workplace share many of the guidelines for a house or an apartment, but in this context there is an extra dimension to encourage a healthy flow of money. The site and design of your business is just as important as the commitment to, and efficiency of, the service it provides to customers or clients. If the business is poorly sited or arranged, prosperity, health, and profits may suffer. If you have positive feng shui in your home, this may help to support your business and vice versa, but weak feng shui in the workplace and at home needs corrective action.

In the following pages, positive sites and features are outlined, as well as suggestions of ways to remedy negative positions and counteract the effect of malign energy. When you are assessing a site, it is important to take into account the nature of the surrounding area as well. If business is already flourishing in a certain area, this is a sign of active and successful chi. However, if the land around your workplace has sluggish chi, your productivity will inevitably be affected—even if the feng shui of your store or office is positive.

How to Analyze Your Office Floor Plan

If you have a private office or study, you can do a personal reading for the layout of that room, or if you have space in an open-plan office, you can take a reading for the area immediately around your desk. The example below deals with an open-plan office, and in this situation use the pa tzu compass that relates to the director, manager, or owner of the business (see pages 32–35).

We used pa tzu compass number 1 (see right) in the reading given below. The element for this compass is water. Work through the example and apply the same technique to your office floor plan using your personal pa tzu compass.

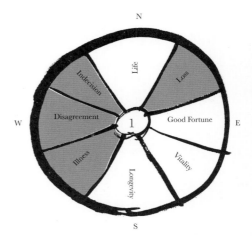

Pa tzu compass 1 • Element: Water

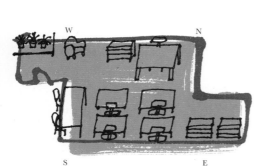

Scale drawing of office floor plan

1 Overlaying your compass Draw a floor plan of your office to scale and overlay the relevant pa tzu compass, as explained on pages 36–37 (see also above and right). Remember to align north on the compass with the northern direction of the office. Or simply use the

compass printed in this book and stand in the center of the office, pointing north on the compass toward north in the office.

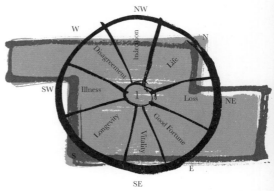

Overlaying your pa tzu compass on your floor plan

The pa tzu compass is associated with only one element, but the eight directions of the room each have their own element. These directions and their associated elements do not change, regardless of where you take a reading.

2 **Assessing the elements** You can see from our floor plan (see page 136) that the four unlucky directions are in the west, northwest, southwest, and northeast, and these are the areas that need attention. Because the element that belongs to pa tzu compass number 1 is water, you will need to find water's relationship with metal and earth—the elements associated with the four unlucky directions in this example (see floor plan, above right). Look at the productive and destructive cycles of the elements shown on the next page.

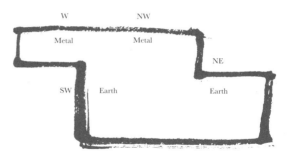

The unlucky directions and their associated elements

3 **Working through unlucky directions** Work through each of your unlucky directions and its relationship with your personal element—in this case, water—one step at a time.

☒ West and northwest fall into the categories of Disagreement and Indecision. The element associated with both these directions is metal. The table on the next page shows that metal produces water.

This is a positive reading, because the two elements complement each other in the creative cycle. Corrective action is not needed, but you can increase the water element by carefully introducing the color black in office equipment or by hanging images that depict water. Or you can increase water by adding a vase of flowers, but be sure that the water does not become stagnant.

☒ Southwest and northeast fall into the categories of Illness and Loss. The element associated with both these directions is earth. The table on the next page shows that earth destroys water.

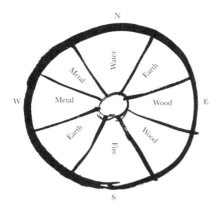

Directions and associated elements

For water to gain strength, the earth element has to be weakened by channeling it toward another element. Because earth creates metal, the introduction of metal colors, textures, and objects will direct earth's energies toward metal. Earth's energy will also be used up as it works to destroy water, and the introduction of a glass vase of flowers, bowls of water, or water images will all strengthen the water element. Finally, if you look at the destructive cycle, you will see that wood destroys earth. The use of plants, small trees, wood textures, or the color green will all diminish the effect of earth, but do not let these destructive combinations become too powerful.

4 **Office layout** The position of desks in an office is important for the productivity of the staff, but above all it is the director's desk that requires particular attention. If the desk belonging to the person who runs the company is in a weak position, the effects can reverberate at all levels of the company. It is also important for staff making financial decisions to be in a secure position where they are not subject to frequent disturbances or a sudden onrush of chi. In this example, the director's desk is in the top right-hand corner, protected on two sides by a wall but not hemmed in by these walls. The person sitting here can see who is entering and leaving the office yet is far enough away from the door to avoid being subject to a surge of energy entering the room. The director's desk falls into the categories of Life and Indecision, but the elemental combinations above can help to improve the weak section. Most of the other desks in the office are placed so that those sitting at them have the support of a wall behind, but the desks in the center of the room need additional support. The room with the printers in the top left-hand corner is screened off to lessen the disruptive impact of noise on the staff and the circulation of chi.

Productive cycle	Destructive cycle
Wood produces fire	Wood destroys earth
Fire produces earth	Earth destroys water
Earth produces metal	Water destroys fire
Metal produces water	Fire destroys metal
Water produces wood	Metal destroys wood

The Site of a Business

Your workplace should be sited according to the nature of the business you want to encourage. If you are dependent upon a regular flow of customers, choose a thriving business area, which is evidence of active chi on that site. It is better to find small premises in a well-established district than large premises in a deserted area. If you rely on a peaceful environment for your work, you should choose a more residential area.

The building that houses your workplace should not be lower in height than neighboring buildings, because the pressure they exert could affect your judgment and creativity. It should also be sited on raised ground to avoid flooding. Be alert to neighboring structures or features, such as the corners of roads or power lines that could cut through the circulation of chi and carry negative energy directly to your premises. You should also assess the buildings that are nearby to see if the four animal guardians are well-balanced, offering your workplace security and protection.

Chi flows smoothly toward this shopping/business center. There are roads leading off the circular approach so chi is not trapped, while the curved shape of the road leading to it enhances the flow of chi. The good fortune drawn to this area is improved because the buildings are of different shapes and heights while still maintaining a harmony in the overall design.

ABOVE A business should not be sited next to a road that has fast and heavy traffic. Chi is dispersed by the rapid movement of the vehicles, and the workers' sense of well-being is disrupted by noise and pollution levels. Use mirrors or springs to deflect or bounce back destructive forces. You can also shield first-floor windows with blinds. The reading is improved if the site is away from the road and has a green area in front of it, producing healthy chi and providing space for clients or employees to walk or sit.

BELOW A quiet street with little traffic can adversely affect business, because the lack of activity deadens business chi. Attract attention by brightly decorating and signposting the front of the building. Create a sense of activity and energy inside a store with moving objects—fans, aquariums, and small fountains. The site may prove productive if the business requires a quiet environment and is not dependent on attracting customers from the street.

The narrow gap between the two buildings siphons the profits away from the business facing it. The gap is likened to a thin slice taken out of a cake. (See advice on page 141.)

The corner of one building facing the main entrance of another has a negative effect, because it resembles a knife slicing into the profits of the business. (See advice on page 141.)

Good feng shui   Bad feng shui   Improved feng shui

The bend of the road is likened to a scythe cutting into the business, weakening the productivity and harmony of the company. (See advice, below right.)

When the road forks opposite the main entrance, it can create confusion and disappointment, because the profits that should be directed into the building are being channeled away. (See advice, below right.)

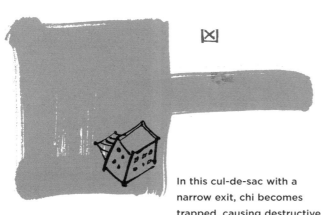

In this cul-de-sac with a narrow exit, chi becomes trapped, causing destructive forces to gather in the angular corners. This weakens the efficiency of the business. Avoid positioning the front door opposite these points. (See advice right.)

• *Advice* In the previous five examples, the main entrance to the business needs strengthening to ward off negative forces. Position a mirror so that destructive energy is sent straight back, or use reflective surfaces to deflect this energy (be careful not to deflect it onto neighbors or back on yourself). Create a screen with blinds or a porch, or move the entrance to the side. Introduce greenery and lights to activate chi. Bounce away negative energy with a spring facing the dangerous corner of an overpowering structure.

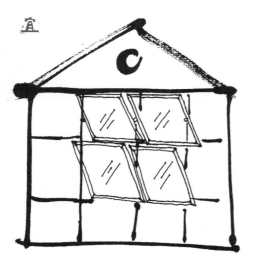

Windows are one way chi enters a building. Reflective glass limits or blocks chi; in turn, this limits the efficiency of those working inside. If windows cannot be opened to let in energy, increase the circulation of chi inside with lights, plants, a fan, or moving water.

If your business faces buildings or structures with a large area of reflective surfaces, such as glass, polished steel, or aluminum, try to block or fracture the reflections by adding features such as awnings, greenery, or balconies.

If you are choosing a site, assess the natural and built features carefully. Avoid low-lying land and garbage depots, where chi is stagnant and sha is present. These factors will adversely affect the health and efficiency of the staff.

Parks, gardens, trees, and shrubs all provide a pleasant and healthy feel to a busy commercial area. They produce healthy chi and ease the pressures created by heavy traffic and crowded pedestrian areas.

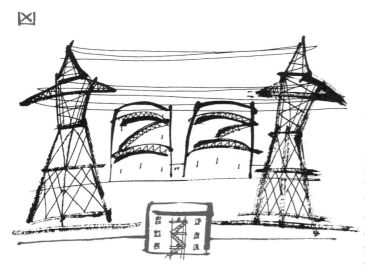

Beware of nearby power stations and derelict sites, and of satellite dishes, antennae, and power lines pointing at the building. Their impact can be bounced away with springs or a mirror; an open pair of scissors placed above the mirror offers extra protection by cutting through the effect of power lines. Sha that travels along power lines or from satellite dishes can also be absorbed with open trays or containers of sand, wood chips, or foam.

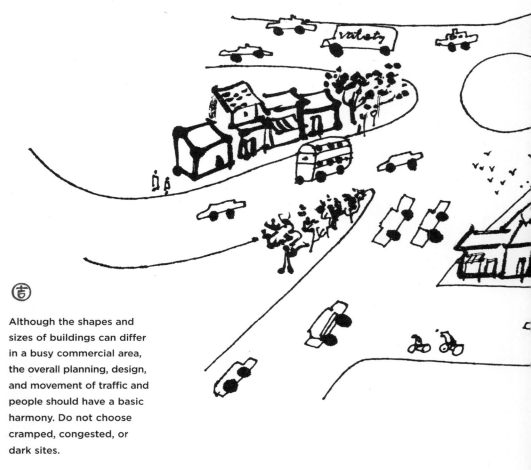

Although the shapes and
sizes of buildings can differ
in a busy commercial area,
the overall planning, design,
and movement of traffic and
people should have a basic
harmony. Do not choose
cramped, congested, or
dark sites.

The intersections of roads and junctions
are usually busy areas that attract positive
business chi. However, if the business is on
the corner of a crossroads (right), the main
entrance should not face one of the opposite
corners. Try to move the entrance to the side
or place a reflective object over the door to
send back any negative forces directed at
the building.

Your workplace should not be dwarfed by other buildings that act like oppressive weights, stunting the growth of your business. Place swordlike objects or springs on the roof to ward off destructive energy.

If the building on the Green Dragon side of your workplace is higher than your building, it should not have a detrimental effect, because the Green Dragon has an active and productive spirit.

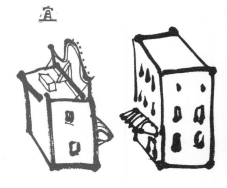

If the building on the White Tiger side is too high, the White Tiger may need to be controlled, because it can rise up and consume the Green Dragon. You can limit its activity by building a roof garden or pool to enliven the chi of your own building, or by placing springs on the roof.

An overpowering building in the position of the Red Bird places pressure on your business. Heighten your building with signs on the roof or by building up the front wall.

A building that towers above its neighbors is isolated, unprotected, and will probably experience the full impact of forceful elements. Use blinds and mirrors to shield the offices, and arrange the layout to maximize energy flow.

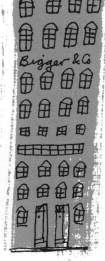

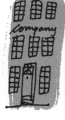

🔯 Good feng shui   ☒ Bad feng shui   ⬛ Improved feng shui

Triangular or blade-shape premises trap destructive energy in their points, but curves help to soften this effect. This problem is difficult to avoid, so be sure internal energy flow is maximized.

Chi rolls quickly off layers or sloping roofs, which is an indication that business success will gradually slip away from you. Curved eaves will catch chi and control its flow.

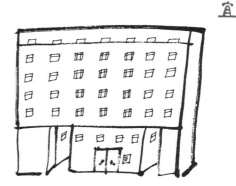

A business needs solid foundations, which supporting pillars cannot provide. The chi in this building is also disturbed by the continual movement of the cars entering and leaving the parking lot. Lack of space means this problem cannot be eliminated entirely, but it can be improved by enlarging and rounding the pillars.

Top-heavy buildings lack support and can also oppress those working at lower levels. The weight from the higher levels may result in divisions being created within the company to alleviate the pressure, place wide, and preferably round, pillars under the unsupported sides of the structure.

Entrance to the Workplace

The area in front of the workplace should be bright and welcoming and the path outside well paved and smooth. A blockage outside the main entrance could divert chi away into neighboring businesses. Clear away waste bags and containers, which are sources of sha, and make sure the entrance to the workplace is well-lit and clearly indicated. Avoid leading customers down dark or cramped paths, because this means they will have passed through an area where chi is limited even before they have made a decision whether to buy your goods or use your services. A clean, bright, well-maintained entrance not only attracts beneficial energy but also creates a positive atmosphere for those who are about to conduct business there. If you rely on the public for your trade, it is particularly important that the main entrance is not obscured from public view.

The main door of a business should be larger than that of a domestic residence to draw customers inside, and it should be slightly higher than street level to limit negative forces entering. It should be wide and well-maintained to encourage chi and create a positive first impression; if the door is small, extra paneling or glass around it can create an illusion of size.

Some premises have more than one entrance; in small businesses this can both confuse customers and divert chi. Ideally, the main access point should be on the Green Dragon side of the building, because this side symbolizes activity. If this is not possible, you should still try to create a main access point by clearly marking one entrance and making it welcoming.

 Good feng shui   Bad feng shui   Improved feng shui

Chi is squeezed when it is channeled swiftly through a narrow porch or has to enter low, cramped doorways. Clear away clutter to maximize access for chi and keep a light on by the door or in the porch.

Cover or move drains and pipes at the front of the building, because they are said to siphon away profits. The main drainage pipes should be at the side or, ideally, at the back of the building.

Large signs or vegetation hanging over the doorway obstruct the flow of beneficial business chi entering the premises. Move the sign above the doorway and cut back the vegetation.

Do not use materials or features that are pointed, angular, or too rough. A facade of rough brick can, however, be used if it is constructed in an even, regular way on the frontage.

A steep flight of steps leading down from the entrance enables profits to roll out of the business. The steps should be graded less steeply and a porch built to prevent chi from escaping. If this is not possible, be sure the door is kept shut and add an inner door to prevent loss of chi.

An awning over the main entrance helps to gather chi and channels it into the business. The awning should be in proportion to the overall size of the building or the entrance itself.

Lobbies, Corridors, and Doors

After beneficial chi enters your building, do not let it become trapped or diverted as a result of the conditions it immediately encounters. If the lobby, foyer, or hallway is spacious, clean, and bright, there is a greater potential for chi to circulate freely. There should be several doors leading off the entrance area to allow for an increased flow of energy to various parts of the building, but avoid stairs or escalators located directly in front of the main entrance. In this position, they provide rapid access for negative forces to the upper floors of the building. Stairs or escalators wll also pull enriching chi away from the first floor.

The foyer should be wide, bright, and welcoming with several doors or exits leading to other parts of the premises, allowing for chi to circulate freely. After chi enters the business, it can become trapped in small dark foyers and will be further limited if there is only one door leading to the rest of the business. In cases such as this, always keep the area well-lit.

 Good feng shui   Bad feng shui   Improved feng shui

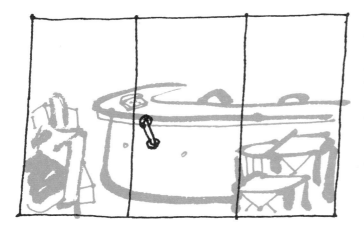

LEFT Do not block the circulation of chi into the building by putting heavy obstacles or furniture in the foyer or reception area. Make sure that wastebaskets are emptied regularly and remove any trash bags to prevent the accumulation of sha.

Your prosperity will be affected if elevator doors face the entrance, because chi is rapidly channeled into the elevator, preventing it from circulating on the first floor. Similarly, stairs opposite the main entrance let negative energy gain easy access. You can use a mirror to reflect back some of the incoming energy, so it can travel in a different direction. If the entrance faces a lavatory, keep the door shut and the area screened with a reception desk or display counter to prevent sha from unbalancing and dissipating incoming chi.

ABOVE **Bright colors, space, light, and a reasonable amount of greenery or number of flowers enhance the feng shui of a lobby or reception area. The gentle movement of a fountain activates chi and draws good fortune into the premises.**

LEFT **The flow of beneficial chi is limited to an office at the end of a long, narrow corridor, while negative forces can be directed like an arrow straight to your door. As a result, your authority or decision-making skills may be weakened. If you cannot change office, hang a small mirror above the door to reflect the oncoming energy.**

ABOVE Avoid choosing an office that faces
a steep staircase or an elevator, because
financial fortune can easily slip away. Keep
the door shut and erect a bookcase or
screen inside the office to prevent excess
chi from escaping.

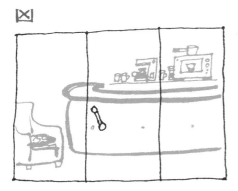

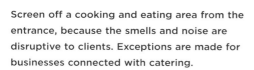

Screen off a cooking and eating area from the
entrance, because the smells and noise are
disruptive to clients. Exceptions are made for
businesses connected with catering.

If offices lead off a long wide corridor, the
corridor should be well-lit, bright, and clean.
Make sure the access to office doors is clear
and that discarded files are removed and
wastebaskets are emptied regularly.

Workplace Layout

The position of your desk can affect your concentration, creativity, and productivity, so you need to find conditions to suit your style of working and the nature of your work. If you are making crucial decisions or keeping accounts, you are advised to sit in a quiet room, away from the main entrance, computer printers, the cafeteria, and any other sources of noise that may disrupt your concentration. If you rely on group work, you may find that it is more conducive to be in a busy, lively office to encourage creativity.

The place where you sit needs good lighting and adequate ventilation to enliven chi. It also needs support; walls, screens, or a piece of furniture behind your chair will offer protection. Try not to put yourself in a vulnerable position, whether it is in the direct line of an open door, escalator, flight of stairs, or next to a large, single-pane glass window, because this will affect your work.

RIGHT **The entrance to a manager's or accounts office should be well-lit, spacious, and clear of trash, because these areas are at the heart of the business. A mistake here could weaken the "limbs" of the business. If these offices are near a lavatory, place an ornamental mirror over the door and a healthy plant nearby to prevent sha from spreading.**

ABOVE RIGHT **Unless the proprietor or director needs regular contact with customers, the director's office should not be seen by the public, because privacy and a quiet atmosphere aid concentration.**

LEFT **If the manager or director shares an open-plan office, his or her desk should be the focal point and situated in the strongest position. The other desks should be arranged evenly around the main desk, allowing for a smooth flow of chi through the room.**

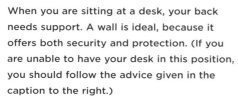

When you are sitting at a desk, your back needs support. A wall is ideal, because it offers both security and protection. (If you are unable to have your desk in this position, you should follow the advice given in the caption to the right.)

A window or open door behind you is known as "the empty door" and your concentration may slip through this space. If you cannot reposition your desk, create a shield with plants, filing cabinets, or a bookcase (do not let files or books jut out above your head).

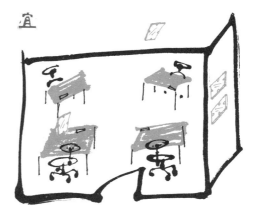

Avoid facing the door, because the incoming chi or malign energy can be too powerful, making it difficult for you to focus on your work or make decisions. In situations such as this, a vase of flowers, a rack for filing papers, and a desk lamp offer a level of protection.

If you are sitting with your back to the door, you can never be sure who is entering or leaving the room. A small mirror on the wall beside or in front of you will enable you to see what is happening behind you and help you feel more in control.

The desk in the corner on the opposite side of the room to the door is in the strongest position, with support at the back and a clear view of who is entering the room without being in direct line of the door. The desk on the right is protected at the back but does not immediately enable the person sitting there to see who is entering.

Desks that are positioned haphazardly and surrounded by clutter create a sense of confusion as well as disrupting the flow of chi over and around the features in the room. Clear the clutter and rearrange the desks to create a more harmonious and balanced working environment.

Many of the people sitting at the desks in this open-plan office are in a vulnerable position, because they have no support behind them and/or are unable to see who is entering the room. The tall screen between the desks slices through the chi and creates a feeling of oppression for those directly facing it, so it should be removed or reduced in size. The desks that have the support of a wall yet still afford a view of movement in and around the office are better protected. The photocopier and printers in the center should be screened off to lessen noise that cuts through the chi of the office.

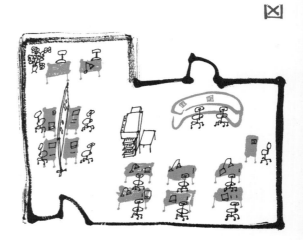

 Good feng shui   Bad feng shui   Improved feng shui

You can improve weak readings by adding protection in certain areas—for example, keeping a blind down to add support to your back, creating a low screen with a bookcase or cabinet, introducing greenery or flowers, and installing bright but not overpowering lights. Small reflective objects will also help to send back negative energy. Finally, you can move your desk on an angle to avoid backing onto weak areas.

If the business is a store or restaurant, the position of the cash registers is especially important. These should be located at a busy point to encourage the flow of money, but they should not face an entrance or doorway, because the money will flow out as readily as it enters.

Checklist

- Can chi circulate freely in and around the office furniture?
- Are wastebaskets emptied regularly and discarded files removed?
- Do you have support or protection when you are sitting at your desk?
- Can you see who is entering or leaving your office or study?
- Does your desk face an open door?
- Is there a window directly behind your chair?
- Is your desk in a dark corner of the office?
- Are you sitting next to noisy computers or other office equipment?
- Is access to the office cramped, poorly lit, or narrow?
- Is the accounts office in a quiet and well-protected area?

Bibliography and Further Reading

de Bary, Theodore (editor), *Sources of Chinese Tradition Vol. I*. New York, NY: Columbia University Press, 1960.

Kwok, Man-Ho, *The Feng Shui Kit: The Chinese Way to Health, Wealth and Happiness, at Home and at Work*. Edited by Joanne O'Brien. First published in 1995 by: Piatkus, London; Charles E. Tuttle Co. Inc., Boston, MA; HarperCollins Publishers, Sydney; Asiapac Books, Singapore.

Kwok, Man-Ho, and Joanne O'Brien, *The Elements of Feng Shui*. Shaftesbury, England/ Rockport, MA: Element Books, 1991.

Kwok, Man-Ho, Martin Palmer, and Jay Ramsay, *The Illustrated Tao Te Ching*. Shaftesbury, England/ Rockport, MA: Element Books, 1993.

Legge, James (translator), *The Chinese Classics Vol. III*. Oxford: Oxford University Press, 1871

(reprinted by Southern Materials Center Inc., Taipei, 1983).

Needham, Joseph (translator), *Science and Civilisation in China Vol. II*. Cambridge: Cambridge University Press, 1956.

Palmer, Martin, Jay Ramsay, and Zhao Xiaomin (translators), *I Ching: The Shamanic Oracle of Change*. London/San Francisco, CA: Thorsons, 1995.

Palmer, Martin and Zhao Xiaomin, *Essential Chinese Mythology*. London/San Francisco, CA: Thorsons, 1997.

Wong, Eva, *Feng Shui: The Ancient Wisdom of Harmonious Living for Modern Times*. Boston, MA: Shambhala, 1996.

Wong, Eva, *The Teachings of the Tao*. Boston, MA: Shambhala, 1997.

Index

Page numbers in *italics* refer to illustrations

Acknowledgments

AUTHOR'S ACKNOWLEDGMENTS
We would like to thank our colleagues and friends at ICOREC for their invaluable support and advice during the preparation of this book. We would also like to express our gratitude to Tessa Monina, Sarah Howerd, and illustrator Meilo So.